PIERRE GOUROU

MAN
AND LAND
IN
THE FAR EAST

Translated from
the French by S. H. BEAVER

LONGMAN
LONDON and NEW YORK

LONGMAN GROUP LIMITED
Burnt Mill
Harlow
Essex CM20 2JE

Distributed in the United States of America by
Longman Inc., New York

*Associated companies, branches and representatives
throughout the world*

English translation © Longman Group Limited, 1975

La terre et l'homme en extrême-orient,
first published 1972 by Flammarion

English edition first published 1975

ISBN 0 582 50240 3

Library of Congress Catalog Card Number: 73–91779

Set in IBM Baskerville, 11 on 12 point

*Printed in Great Britain by
Whitstable Litho Ltd*

Man and land in the Far East

CONTENTS

LIST OF FIGURES

EDITOR'S PREFACE

Pierre Gourou, described by one of his former colleagues as 'a reincarnation of Vidal de la Blache', was professor at the Collège de France in Paris, where from 1947 to 1971 he gave regular courses of lectures on tropical geography. At the same time he held a professorship in the Free University of Brussels. He was loved and admired in both cities and by the professional geographers of both countries. Some of his former pupils and colleagues in Paris encouraged him to publish, in 1971, *Leçons de géographie tropicale*, a résumé of the various courses that he had delivered at the Collège de France; whilst in 1970 his colleagues in Belgium honoured him on his retirement by the publication of a volume of his papers — *Receuil d'articles: hommage de la Société royale belge de Géographie au Prof. P. Gourou*. The latter volume, of 450 pages, contains twenty-eight separate articles, no less than twenty of which are concerned with tropical geography.

Prof. Gourou's tropical fieldwork was intensive and far flung, in three continents. In the 1930s he spent much time in French Indo-China, and in the 1950s he was active in the Belgian Congo. His researches in southeast Asia led to three major publications — *Le Tonkin* (Paris, 1931), *Les paysans du Delta tonkinois* (Paris, 1936) and *L'utilisation du sol en Indochine française* (Paris, 1940); whilst his whole tropical study and experience culminated in his major work, *Les Pays tropicaux*, in 1947, which, as *The Tropical World*, appears in the 'Geographies for Advanced Study' series (4th edition, largely re-written, 1966). Other textbooks have flowed from his pen, including *L'Asie* (1950, revised 1971), *L'Afrique* (1970) and *Géographie Humaine* (1973).

The present work was originally published in Paris in 1940, but the French publisher Flammarion regarded it as of such current importance in the understanding of the Far Eastern situation that it was re-issued in 1972, much revised and with a new concluding chapter on changes during the last thirty years. It is true that the greater part of the book relates to the historical development of man—land relationships in eastern Asia and to conditions as Prof. Gourou knew them in the 1930s. But its penetrating analysis of human geography is an indispensable foundation for the study of more recent developments. Prof. Gourou analyses the remarkable changes that have taken place in China and in Japan; alas, the situation in Vietnam and its neighbouring states is still not stabilised sufficiently to enable comparable judgments to be made.

'The geographer needs a multiplicity of endowments, and those, indeed, of the rarest kind. He must be able to glimpse what is not readily apparent, to register fully what is accessible to the eye, and to commit to memory what he has observed; but also to work ahead of his observation, thus grasping its true impact. For his cautious investigations, he must also be able to draw upon all the humane disciplines, including those, the oldest, which are firmly established and developed, and those which are as yet only in their infancy. He must be anthropologist, historian, demographer, sociologist, all rolled into one. Pierre Gourou's quest for knowledge takes all these directions; all these ancillary skills, all these techniques, are weapons in his academic armoury' (Fernand Braudel in the Preface to the *Leçons*). All his skills, descriptive and interpretative, are brought to bear on this study of man's response to the environment of eastern Asia — a total environment that over the centuries owes as much to man himself as to the physical forces that created it.

S. H. BEAVER

University of Keele
March 1974

CHAPTER 1

THE FAR EAST

The peasant lands of the Far East have spawned, during the last few thousand years, human populations that have developed into the nations of China, Korea, Japan and Vietnam. These nations are evolving at different paces, becoming increasingly urban and industrialised; but they owe their human strength to the capitalisation, over many centuries, of the surplus peasant populations. The purpose of this book is to examine the human geography of these Far Eastern countries as it was before the economic revolution that is taking place before our very eyes. It is a human geography that is very far from being obsolete, for the Far Eastern countrysides are like a parchment that still bears the scratches of its ancient text.

From the southernmost point of the Mekong delta to the confluence of the Amur and the Usuri, the peasants show a physical kinship, settle in villages, seek out the alluvial plains, and ignore hills and mountains; though they are very poor pastoralists they practise an agriculture that is both arduous and skilful; they discovered tea and silk; they feed almost exclusively on vegetable products, and clothe themselves in vegetable fibres; their tools, like their houses, are made of wood and bamboo. Throughout the Far East there is a remarkable similarity of agricultural techniques, and a low standard of life. Families are organised on a common model. Religious beliefs are similar, with an agrarian animism that appears beneath a varnish of Buddhism, Taoism or Confucianism. Higher modes of thought were largely of Chinese

Fig. 1.1   General map of the Far East. The names of the traditional eighteen provinces of China are given in bold type

origin, and children were taught to understand Chinese characters.

The homogeneity of this peasantry is a feature of Far Eastern civilisation. Among an ethnic stock that was common to both the Far East and Indonesia, Chinese civilisation flourished; it spread easily southwards, and its progress was arrested only when it came into contact with another advanced civilisation, emanating from India; and indeed it actually encroached upon the territory formerly occupied by that civilisation. The relief of the Far East presents no barriers to north—south movement and relationships; the summers are equally warm and wet over thirty degrees of latitude, thus leading to an agricultural uniformity without necessarily imposing it.

In 1930, 400 million peasants lived in the Far East, representing four-fifths of the total population of this part of the world. Today, the peasants may number 600 million, though now only forming three-fifths of the total population. Such a mass of rural humanity cannot but attract our attention.

The eastern flank of Asia stands out clearly as a region because of its climate and its Chinese civilisation. It differs from the Indian subcontinent and contrasts markedly with the semi-arid lands of central Asia. Within the Far East, comprising Vietnam, China, Korea and Japan, the peasant and urban populations together number 1000 million, or well over a quarter of all mankind.

Modern air travel no longer allows the appreciation of the diversity of landscapes that used to confront the traveller from Europe to eastern Asia. Leaving behind the moderately populated arable areas and the animal-rearing pastures of northwest Europe, he would first encounter the Mediterranean landscapes with their sparsely vegetated slopes and rocky mountains; then the Suez Canal, the shores of the Red Sea and ports of call such as Djibouti or Aden, desert jewels. In Ceylon, tropical vegetation and a new ethnic type conditioned the traveller to appreciate the characteristics of Singapore. Colombo is essentially Indian, but the Chinese city of Singapore ushers in the Far East. It is only an outpost, however; the Malay Peninsula is but moderately peopled, and Chinese are found side by side with Malays and Indians, while vast plantations are evidence of a European technology.

At Saigon the traveller is definitely in the Far East — and he would remain so until he reached Siberia. The Saigon—Cholan urban area reminds one of Singapore; but with the difference that in Saigon the countryside and the city form a coherent whole. The same Vietnamese who live in the city people the countryside. A whole new world appears in the rural landscape, in the customs (such as the conduct of funerals or the use of

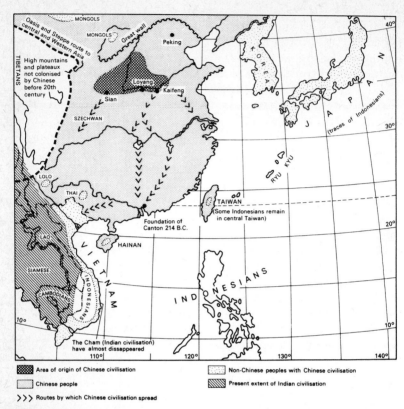

Fig. 1.2   Chinese civilisation in the Far East

chopsticks at meals), in the architecture and decoration of
temples, and in the use of Chinese writing. A rapid journey into
Cambodia helps to strengthen this strong and vivid impression.
For Cambodia is profoundly different; the land is less carefully
treated, the boundaries of the cultivated fields are less clear;
many areas are under-utilised, even in the areas of dense population; cattle are more numerous; houses are built on poles, while
those in Vietnam are set on the ground. The Cambodians are very
different in their civilisation from the Vietnamese, and the
boundary between the Indian world and that of the Far East
passes between Cambodia and Vietnam. There is something of an
antipathy between the two peoples; it is very unfortunate for the
Cambodians that recent political developments have subjected

their country to the intervention and extortions of both North and South Vietnamese, whom the Cambodians regard as their traditional enemies.

To go overland from South Vietnam to the port of Fusan in Korea, whence one may embark for Japan, is to traverse the whole of the continental Far East: the plains of Annam and the Red River confirm the first impressions gained at Saigon; rice-fields everywhere, few cattle and no pastures; human beings with yokes are the bearers of burdens; handcarts, common in Cambodia, have disappeared; low houses are gathered in villages that are concealed by bamboos and dominated by the solid mass of a temple with a cornute spire.

Such are the characteristic traits of the rural countryside of the Far East; they are found, with but minor variations, over the whole of this vast region. It is the background to the civilisations that is responsible for this homogeneity. In going from south to north the traveller encounters nothing of the range of climates that he experienced on his journey from Europe. No desert, no Mediterranean climate intervenes between the tropical and temperate zones; in summer, which is the rainy season, the vegetation is equally luxuriant at Saigon, Shanghai, Peking and Hakodate.

CHAPTER 2

A CLIMATIC UNITY

The idea that everything is a matter of chance is one
that the Wise Men invented for inferior intelligences.

Hung Liang Chi (18th century)

TEMPERATURE[1]

Since the Far East stretches for 4500 km, from Point Camau
(Cape Cambodia) in latitude 10°N to the Amur River and the
north coast of Hokkaido in latitude 50°N, there are naturally
great temperature differences between the northern and southern
ends (Figs. 2.4 and 2.5).

Differences due to latitude are reinforced by the occurrence of
the monsoons: in winter polar continental airmasses blow across
eastern Asia towards the 'Inter-Tropical Convergence Zone'
which lies about 10 degrees south of the equator (Fig. 2.3). In
summer, on the other hand, the disposition of the Asiatic coastline and the action of ocean currents cause the ITCZ to shift far
to the north and to the east, thus opening up the Far East to a
general flow of warm, southerly air of oceanic origin and high
humidity (Figs. 2.1 and 2.2). It is this that is responsible for the
very remarkable temperature range experienced at Harbin (43
degrees: compare London 13 and Paris 14).

Winters in the north, under the influence of the continental
interior of Siberia, are very cold (Fig. 2.6); and even at Hanoi the
winter is slightly cooler than the latitude would suggest. The
Annamite ranges, elongated from northwest to southeast through
eastern Indochina, are something of a climatic barrier; their

---

[1] All temperatures are shown in °C.

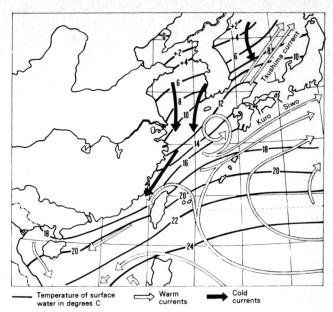

Temperature of surface water in degrees C → Warm currents → Cold currents

Fig. 2.1   Sea temperatures and ocean currents in January

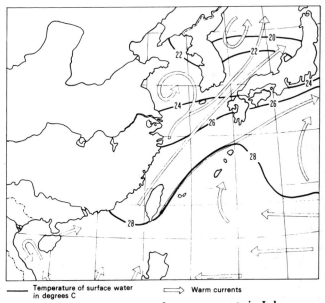

Temperature of surface water in degrees C → Warm currents

Fig. 2.2   Sea temperatures and ocean currents in July

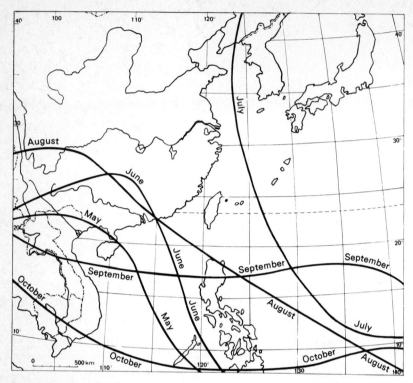

Fig. 2.3 The inter-tropical convergence zone: mean monthly positions between May and October (after J. F. Flores and V. F. Balagot, in *World Survey of Climatology*, viii, Amsterdam, 1969, 169)

eastern side is still subject to the cooling influence on the winter monsoon, while the western side of the range on the same latitude is warmer; so the maritime (Vietnamese) side has a cooler winter than the continental (Laotian) side. Further south, such differences are obliterated, and Saigon has temperatures that are normal for its tropical latitude; the hottest month is April, which is usual for latitude 10°N. At Hanoi the hottest month is June, and further north, July.

The uniformity of the hot season is a marked and unique characteristic of the Far East; although Saigon and Mukden are separated by 31 degrees of latitude (almost as great a distance as from London to Timbuktu), their mean July temperatures differ by only 2.5 degrees (and at Saigon July is not the hottest

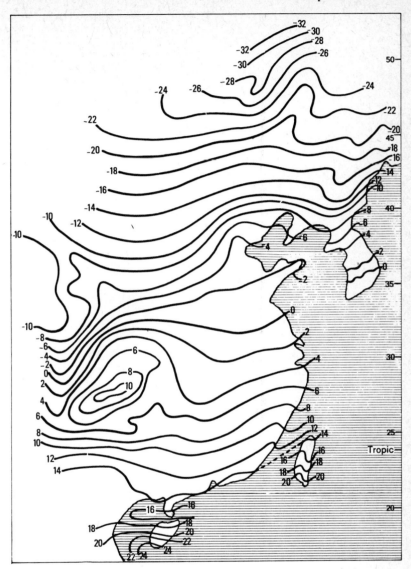

Fig. 2.4   **Actual mean temperatures in January**

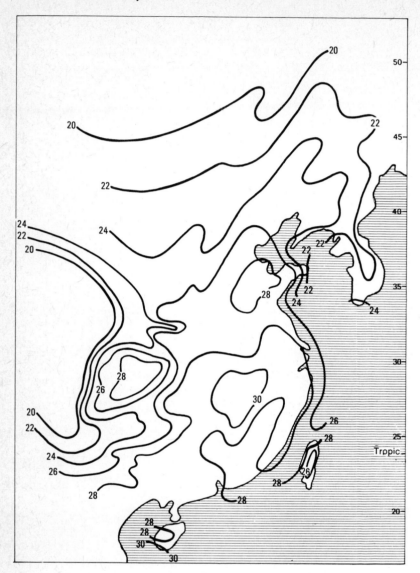

Fig. 2.5   Actual mean temperatures in July

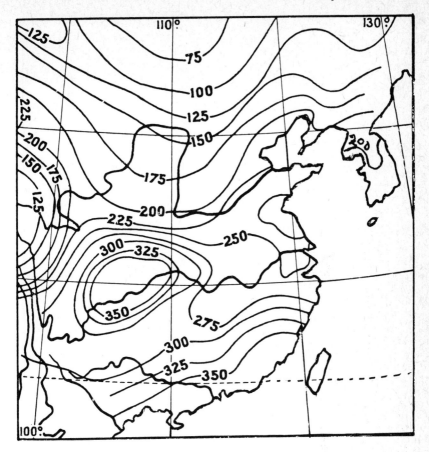

Fig. 2.6   Mean duration of frost-free period

month). Mukden, at 42°N, has a July mean of 24.9°C, Saigon, at 10°N, a mean of 27.4°C. So in July one cannot escape the heat by travelling north in the Far East; coolness is only attainable through altitude. But the island of Hokkaido, and particularly its northeastern side, does escape the great heat; here (e.g., at Nemuro) there are cool fogs that give almost a subpolar feel to the climate. Only through the hard work and skill of the Japanese has rice cultivation been developed in such an environment.

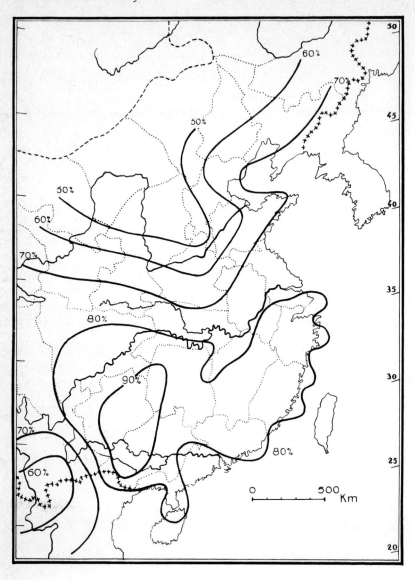

Fig. 2.7   Mean annual relative humidity in China

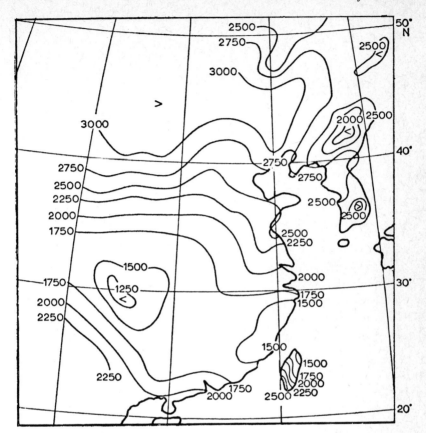

Fig. 2.8   Mean annual sunshine total, in hours (after H. Arakawa, in *World Survey of Climatology*, viii, 36)

RAINFALL

The summer monsoon, with its gush of warm, humid, southerly air, is responsible for the general summer warmth. It also brings the abundant rains that are the lifeblood of agriculture. The least watered areas are basins and valleys that lie athwart the rain-bearing winds — such as the plain of Phan Thiet in Vietnam (Fig. 2.12), and the area around the Japanese Inland Sea; but these are tiny exceptions to the general pluviosity of the entire Far East. Rainfall in China decreases towards the northwest, and the limit of reliable cropping approximates to the 400 mm isohyet, a

Locality	Lat.°N	Mean temp. of coldest month	Mean temp. of hottest month	Range of monthly means
Harbin	46	−20.1	23.3	43.4
Mukden	42	−12.8	24.9	37.7
Nemuro	43	−5.6	17.5	23.1
Peking	40	−4.7	26.1	30.8
Niigata	38	+1.7	25.8	24.1
Tokyo	35	3.7	26.4	22.7
Ruwanoto	33	4.6	27.0	22.4
Shanghai	31	3.4	27.2	23.8
Canton	23	13.6	28.8	15.2
Hanoi	21	17.2	29.2	12.0
Saigon	10	25.8	28.8	3.0

(For graphs of Peking and Shanghai see Fig. 2.13)

line that roughly follows the Great Wall (Fig. 2.9).

The general rule of a summer maximum of rainfall is exemplified to perfection in northern China and Manchuria, in southern China, and in North and South Vietnam. Some exceptions to the complete dominance of summer precipitation are found in the lower Yangtse basin of China (Figs. 2.10 and 2.11) and in southern Japan, where there are winter and spring rains brought by eastward-moving depressions; also in central Annam, where there are winter rains associated with humid airmasses responding to depressions that stagnate over the China Sea; while the western side of Nippon, facing the Sea of Japan, actually has its maximum rainfall in winter, derived from the northwest monsoon that has become moist during its sea passage.

The rains are augmented, at the end of the summer, by typhoons. These cyclonic storms, coming from the east, ravage the coastal areas of the Far East north of about lat. 12° and are particularly devastating over Taiwan and Japan (Fig. 2.14). In the interior, the typhoons, bringing more rain without so much violent wind, are a more beneficent influence.

VEGETATION

There is relatively little vegetational variation because of the remarkable coincidence of high summer temperatures and high

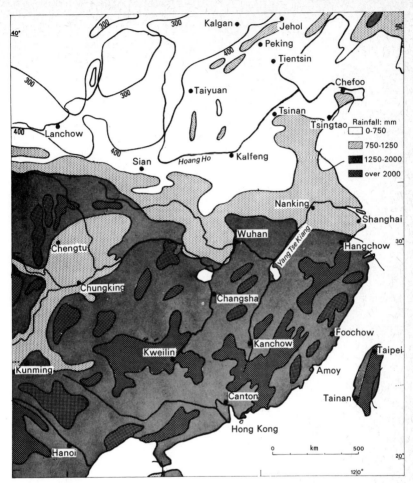

Fig. 2.9 Rainfall in China (after H. von Wissmann, 'Durchsnittliche Nieder-schlagshöhe des jahres', *Zeitschrift des Gesellschaft für Erdkunde zu Berlin*, 1937). Note the contrast between the north (north of the 750 mm isohyet) and the south; also the influence of relief on rainfall

rainfall over the whole length of the Far East — a climatic feature that allows southern species to penetrate far to the north. The flora is rich and varied (15 000 species of grain and forage plants in China) and is a mixture of southern and northern species; plants like tea and oil-yielding camellias are found in all latitudes.

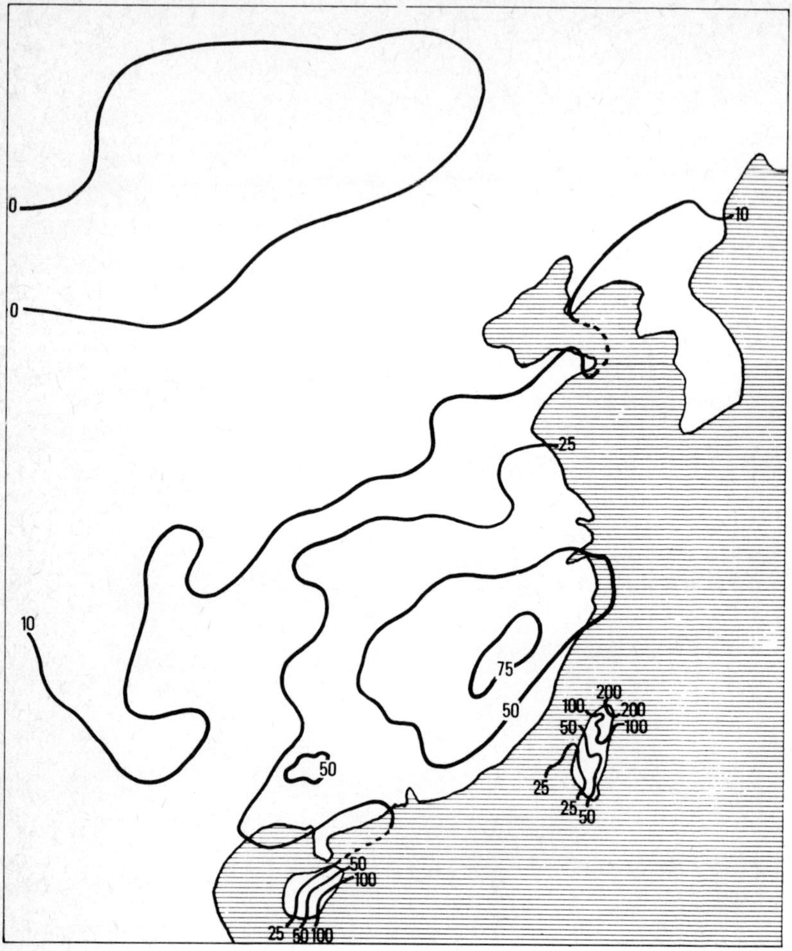

Fig. 2.10   Average rainfall in January

Very ancient species, the ancestors of the Californian sequoias, have been found still living in remote parts of eastern Szechwan. Bamboos are present even as far north as central Japan; rice is cultivated in Manchuria and in Hokkaido, and if it occupies a less important place in northern China this is only because the permeability of the loess is unfavourable to crops that need flood-

Fig. 2.11   Average rainfall in July

ing. However, rice is grown in special circumstances, as in the environs of Peking and of Tai Yuan (in Shansi) and in northern Korea. Wheat is cultivated as far north as Fukien. The forests of northern Vietnam contain oaks and chestnuts, plum trees flourish as far south as the eighteenth parallel. Conifers, which in the tropics are generally confined to the mountains, almost reach

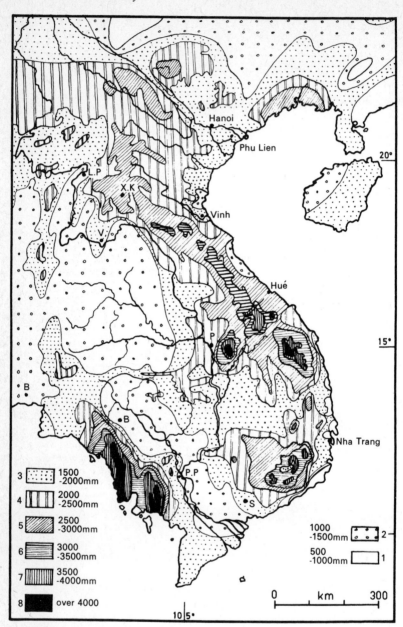

Fig. 2.12   **Annual rainfall in Indochina**

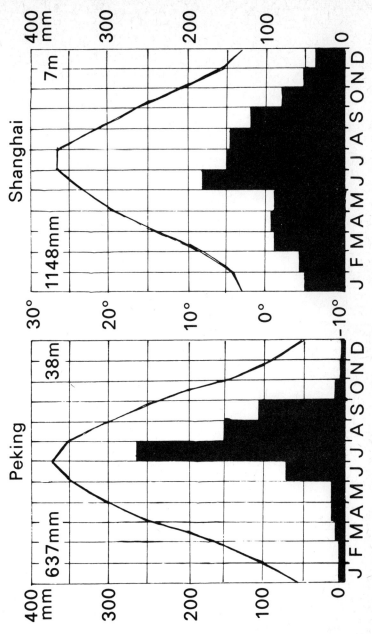

Fig. 2.13 Climatic graphs for Peking and Shanghai

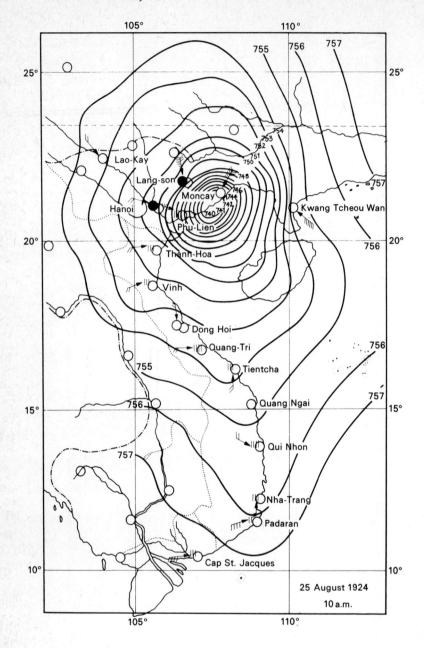

25 August 1924

10 a.m.

the sea in the neighbourhood of Hué in lat. 17°. In this entirely tropical latitude there are also steep hillsides covered with pine, that have provided a motif for Chinese painters and give an unforgettable charm to the countryside of Hué. This heavenly landscape accompanies the Far East to its uttermost limits. There are also stands of pine at low altitude some 50 km north of Kompong Thom in Cambodia, only 13 degrees north of the equator.

The deciduous forests of Korea and northern Japan include, among an immense variety, many species that are closely allied to those of Europe (oak, beech, walnut, maple). The forest is of an astonishing and almost equatorial luxuriance, with an abundance of climbing plants (such as wistaria) and epiphytes.

The climatic continuity of the Far East has permitted the growth, over a vast area and in the tropical as well as the temperate zone, of a uniform civilisation. The same techniques of rice cultivation can be used in northern Korea and in the Mekong delta; the bamboo, throughout the area, has provided a raw material with many uses. But the climatic continuity has merely permitted all this; it was not inevitable. The homogeneity of Far Eastern civilisation results above all from human circumstances.

Fig. 2.14 **A typhoon in the China Sea. Map scale 1/12M. A typhoon, with central barometric pressure of 740 mm, has struck the coast of Tonkin. The strongest winds are from north and east, where the isobars are closest. At Cape St Jacques the winds are blowing in their normal direction. (See Bruzon and Carton, *Le Climat de l'Indochine et les typhons de la Mer de Chine*, 1930, 278.)**

CHAPTER 3

A CULTURAL REGION

The quality of our country towers above savage and
far-off lands. Its way of life is higher than that of Yao
and Chouen. People come from all directions to pay
homage; across the four seas they come to visit our
Emperor.

Pien Tchang (9th century AD)

A FAR EASTERN RACE?

Is there a Far Eastern race? From our early reading and teaching
we have generally come to think of the Far East as the home of
the 'yellow race'. Our conception of a Chinese is of someone
with high cheekbones, a flat nose, slit-like eyes, a thin black
moustache, and yellow colouring. The ordinary Westerner cannot
distinguish a Chinese from a Japanese, or a Korean, or a Vietnamian — they are all just 'yellow'. But would he not also con-
fuse Far Eastern people with Siamese, Burmans, Laotians,
Cambodians or Malays?
  Certain physical traits are particularly widespread throughout
the Far East: the skin colour, black hair, thick and straight, a
hairless body, the 'mongolian' eye (in the inner corner of the eye,
the upper eyelid passes over the lower, so that the caruncle is not
visible), prominent cheekbones, small and slender hands and feet,
short stature and, in youth, a blue spot in the lumbar region. But
when we attempt to give greater precision to these characters and
define their geographical localisation, the doubts multiply. The
skin colour shows some variability; wavy hair is not exceptional;
eyes are not always slit-like; stature varies from region to region,
and in general increases from south to north; the cephalic index
is by no means constant, and the cranial capacity varies from one

country to another, and as between individuals. The Japanese have an exceptional cephalic volume, the Thay (who dwell on the boundary of China and Indochina) the lowest. Blood group classification does not show uniformity either; the north Chinese, the Koreans, and the south Chinese belong to different groups, while Japanese blood closely resembles that of the south Chinese.

There is thus no Far Eastern race, but a population derived from numerous ancient stocks. The remains of *Sinanthropus pekinensis* (Peking man) and *Pithecanthropus javanensis* (Java man) date at least from the middle Pleistocene. Recent archaeological discoveries in various parts of China have revealed human remains of greater antiquity than Peking man. The Far East, by reason of its coastal situation, has had connections both with the Asiatic interior and with Indonesia, and has undoubtedly received peoples of diverse racial origin. The Ainus, an ancient group that some anthropologists regard as of palaeo-Siberian affinities while others point to a possible Polynesian origin, have contributed racial material to Japan, which has also received Indonesian, Korean, Tungus and Chinese elements – diverse ancestry, indeed, for the population of an island that nature would apparently have destined as an area of racial simplicity. The ancestral linkages of the Far Eastern people with the Indonesians, the Thay, and the peoples of Manchuria, Mongolia and Siberia are certain. It is indeed possible to suggest that the ethnological base was of Indonesian affinities, and that this was overlaid by 'Mongoloid' arrivals from the north.

Just as there is no 'Far Eastern' race, so there are really no Chinese, Korean, Japanese or Vietnamese races. There is also linguistic variety: the four languages are very different, not in the way that the members of the Indo-European language group differ from one another, but as, for example, Finnish differs from Swedish, or Turkish from Greek.

Anyone familiar with the Far East might perhaps recognise a Japanese 'type', or a Korean type, several Chinese types, and one or more Vietnamese types. But it would be just as difficult to define one of these types as to define a French type or an English type, even though we think that these exist. Such types result in part from civilisation and behaviour.

ORIGINS OF THE FAR EASTERN WORLD

The Far East has really acquired its homogeneous cultural land-scape through the predominant influence of high Chinese civilisa-tion. And besides, this culture has covered a region that already possessed some degree of homogeneity. Of very ancient origin are certain so-called 'instinctive' habits or gestures (they can hardly be instinctive since they have to be learned by each individual) that are completely opposite to our own. For example, in peeling a fruit, the Far Eastern will push the skin away from him instead of pulling it towards himself; and whereas a European will thread a needle by pushing the end of the thread towards the eye, the Far Eastern will hold the thread still and bring the needle's eye to it. And in the Far East left is more important than right; and the Chinese mount a horse from the right and not from the left.

In pre-Chinese times, central and southern China would appear to have had strong cultural links with southeast Asia. Recent archaeological discoveries in Thailand would seem to indicate that peas, beans (*Dolichos*), cucumbers, water-caltraps were already being grown 9500 years BC, or 2000 years earlier than the most ancient cultivations discovered in the Fertile Crescent or in Mexico. Other studies have shown that rice may have been grown in Thailand about 3500 BC. It is not certain that the traces of rice found with pottery indicate flooded rice, but the size of the grains is clear proof that it was cultivated and not wild rice. This date is earlier than the most ancient rice-growing known in China and India. Thailand has also produced a bronze socketed hatchet of about 1500 BC, much earlier than the first known Chinese bronzes. It is perhaps not imprudent to suggest that Chinese civilisation, expanding from north to south, covered and assimilated a civilisation that had already occupied the Far East.

CHINESE CIVILISATION

Chinese unity is based on unity of civilisation. The average height of the southern Chinese people is 1609 mm, and of the northern Chinese, 1655 mm. In the single province of Fukien there are

108 dialects, many of them mutually unintelligible. Northern China and the Yangtse basin present many different features. Marco Polo, who had no preconceived ideas on the matter, was so much struck by these differences that he gave the two regions different names: Cathay (north China) and Manji (the Yangtse area). The division between the two Chinas coincides roughly with the Hwai basin. To the north, dry cultivation of wheat and sorghum predominates, while to the south lie flooded ricefields. The peasants north of the Hwai River use carts for rural transport, while those to the south labour under yokes and use sampans for heavy loads. The northern cultivator sows his grain in aligned furrows rather than broadcast, and does not use human urine as a fertiliser. However, despite all these physical differences, and the variety of techniques, the unity of China is not in doubt.

From a homeland in northern China, in the middle Hoang Ho basin, Chinese civilisation spread southwards, via the Hwai into the lower Yangtse and by the Nanyang pass and the Han into the middle Yangtse, thence further south to the limits of Kwangtung (Fig. 1.2). In this way, it created a numerous and homogeneous nation, spread over a vast territory and organised as a state, before such a thing had happened in any other part of the world (Fig. 3.1).

It is not surprising that this vast and populous nation, armed with an advanced and efficient civilisation, exercised a powerful influence over all the surrounding countries, either by conquest or by the activities of traders and of Buddhist missionaries, and through the example that it offered to visiting foreigners. In this way Korea, Japan and Vietnam acquired Chinese civilisation and joined with the Celestial Empire to form the Far East.

THE PEOPLING QUALITY OF CHINESE CIVILISATION

The traditional Chinese civilisation strongly favoured the process of settlement, and it encouraged, by a process that will be examined later on, a great density of rural population. It was responsible for the creation of new human landscapes, characterised by the total numbers of people as well as by their density in

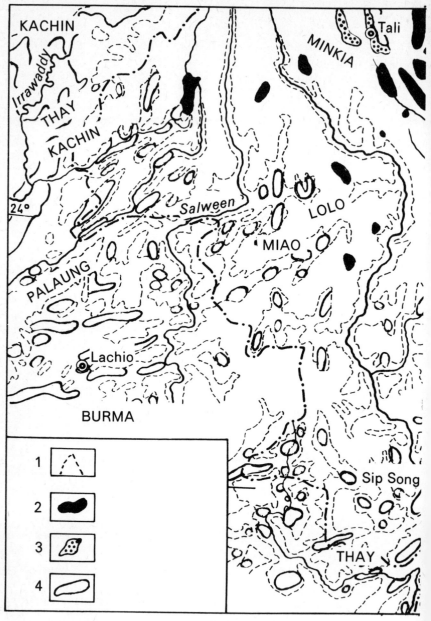

Fig. 3.1   The contact of Chinese and non-Chinese in southwestern China (after H. von Wissmann. *Süd-Yünnan als Teilraum Südostasiens*, Heidelberg, 1943, 28).

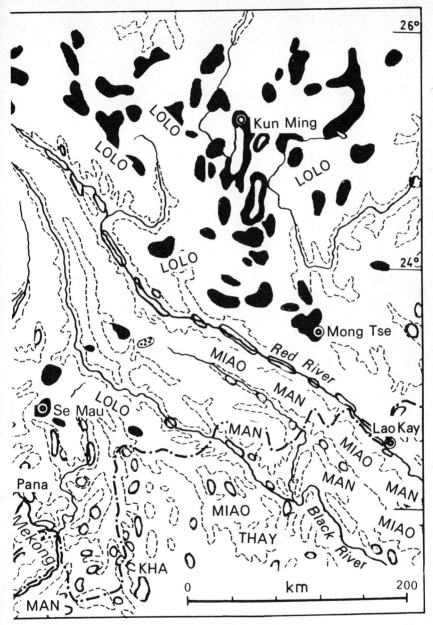

Key: 1. contour of 1300 m, approximate limit of the warmer lands or 'tierra caliente'; 2. basin occupied by Chinese; 3. basin occupied by Min Kia; 4. basin occupied by Thay

Fig. 3.2   A bamboo raft on the Yangtse (from an aerial photograph of 1938)

relation to the cultivated areas. In addition, it gave the peasants the intellectual equipment and the technical framework of an advanced civilisation. As a result, when the modern technological era arrived, the Far Eastern peoples were readily able to understand and master the new techniques that were offered them; on the other hand, effectively enclosed as they were within the framework of their civilisation, they were perfectly conditioned to follow the impulses that this framework provided.[1] Chinese bureaucracy was a very restrictive influence. Organised power and political ideas gave the classical Chinese an enormous

---

[1] This is not the place to cavil at the technological backwardness of Chinese civilisation with regard to that of Europe in the early nineteenth century. In fact this backwardness was not of long standing, and dates only from the late seventeenth century. Before this, Chinese technology was just as advanced as European.

capacity for getting things done. During the period of the Han dynasty, government officials were much concerned with taxes and compulsory labour, and in an effort to secure an equitable imposition, they devised a system of calculation designed to lighten the load of the taxpayer and the length of his service. At the same time, however, this administrative and political machine was capable of requisitioning enormous masses of labour for great works. Chinese documentary sources show that in AD 605–606 the imperial government conscripted 2 million workers to construct the city of Lo Yang, capital of the east. Each of the labourers served for one month. Such a displacement of manpower gives some idea of the efficiency of the technical framework of the ancient Chinese civilisation. And other examples could be quoted: thus in 192 BC 146 000 workers were recruited for the construction of the city of Chang Ngan (Si Ngan), and in 190 BC a further 145 000 for the same purpose; in AD 555 1.8 million conscripts helped to rebuild part of the Great Wall, and in AD 607 a further 1 million for the same purpose; while in AD 1351 150 000 were conscripted for building dykes along the Yellow River.[1]

A VEGETABLE CIVILISATION

The effects of the civilisation are to be seen in every technique of agriculture and craftsmanship, in the localisation of the population in swarms on the plains, in domestic architecture, in the means of transport and in the organisation of society and state. Chinese civilisation has done much to spread that peasant wisdom that has contributed so much to the maintenance of dense rural populations. Two fundamental Chinese axioms are, 'Do what you can, be satisfied with your lot, and follow the climatic seasons', and 'Be in tune with nature'.

The entire Far East has what might be called a 'vegetable civilisation'. Chinese, Japanese and Vietnamians eat very little meat and neglect the use of milk. Clothing is derived from the

[1] L. S. Yang, *Les Aspects économiques des travaux publics dans la Chine impériale*, Paris, 1964.

Fig. 3.3   A Chinese wheelbarrow (from R. H. Hommell, *China at Work*, 1937, 321). Its great virtue is that all the weight is on the iron-rimmed wooden axle. The axle is not oiled, and emits a frightful screech. It can carry enormous loads, e.g., six people and all their luggage. Pulled by either a man or a horse, it may sometimes raise a sail to make use of a following wind

vegetable world. To protect himself from the winter cold the Chinese uses not wool but cotton coats and dresses of lined cotton, piled on in increasing layers as the temperature drops. The soles of his shoes are made not of leather but of esparto grass or layers of cotton. His house is built of wood and bamboo with a thatched roof; stones, cob and mud bricks are used as secondary materials only in northern China. No metal at all enters into the structure, the various parts of which are joined together not with nails or screws, but with wooden joints or ties of bamboo and rattan.

Tools make but a minimal use of metal or other mineral substances; most containers are neither metal nor ceramic, but of basket-work covered with an impermeable coating. Handcarts (Fig. 3.3), which are masterpieces of ingenuity (the weight rests exclusively on the axle and not partly on the arms of the carter), likewise use little or no metal. Ploughs have but a tiny shoe, and spades usually have but a small iron plate. In 1935, China consumed a hundred times less iron, per head of population, than the United Kingdom.

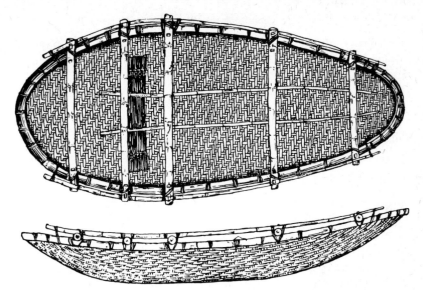

Fig. 3.4 **Small boat made from woven bamboo, on the Red River delta** (after J. Hornell, *Water Transport*, 1946, 110). It measures 1.75 m in length, and is propelled by paddles

THE USE OF BAMBOO

Having bamboo available — or rather, having had the ingenuity to perceive the virtues of bamboo — Chinese technology has derived much profit from it. Bamboo is not unknown in black Africa, but the traditional techniques of tropical Africa have made little use of it. In the Far East bamboo provides yokes for carrying burdens, it is used for poles, scaffolding, pipes, conduits, blinds, in the making of boats, chairs, tables, shelves, boxes, sieves, brooms and brushes, combs, ladders, flexible yardsticks, bows and arrows, umbrella ribs, gates and barriers, posts, stakes, mats, hats, baskets, lanterns and torches, fans, chopsticks, cages for birds and animals, musical pipes, sandals, and bellows pipes for forges; a pipe of green bamboo, filled with rice and thrown on to a fire, gives a dish cooked to perfection when the bamboo dries out; young bamboo shoots are a much-used vegetable; the leaves make excellent forage. Bamboos are a frequent motif in painting, and decorative arts have given expression to the supple, curving stems and the quivering leaves. The bamboo is one of the three plants used as a charm in Japan, because it is the most useful; the others are the pine (the most important construction material) and the plum (because it flowers earliest) (Figs. 3.2 and 3.4).

CLIMATIC AREA AND CULTURAL AREA

The climatic area of the Far East is almost exactly coincident with the cultural area. The only noticeable divergence is in the south, where although the Far Eastern climate (characterised by a greater range of temperature between the hottest and coldest months than the latitude would warrant, and by the incidence of typhoons) extends no further than Cape Varella (lat. 13°N), civilisation of Chinese type extends into southern Annam and the delta of the Mekong. This extension of Far Eastern culture is due to the greater efficiency of Vietnamian techniques, derived from the Chinese, in production and organisation (Fig. 1.2).

Towards the west the frontier, dominated by the plateau of Tibet, was formerly very marked, though it has tended to disappear of late owing to the vigorous Chinese colonisation policy in all the habitable parts of Chinese central Asia. The rigours of the Siberian climate limit the expansion of Far Eastern culture northwards. The agricultural technology of the Chinese encountered an insuperable obstacle in the length and severity of the winter; in a climate more suited to grass than to grain, rural land use had perforce to be concerned with cattle-raising, and the Chinese peasantry was ill-prepared for such a change. Moreover, the political situation, in the basins of the Liao and Sungari rivers, was for a long time hardly propitious for Chinese colonisation; for this area, as far as the Amur River, was part of the Japanese protectorate of Manchuria. This explains why, when the Russian west—east expansion through Siberia took place, it could reach the Pacific without encountering a rural population in the Far Eastern style.

APTITUDE AND RESISTANCE TO CHANGE

Japan modernised itself much earlier than China, for the authorities willed the change in 1868. The intellectual and technological

potential present in Japan through its Chinese civilisation encountered no official opposition after that date, to the assimila-
tion of Western ideas. But China floundered, its higher authorities
rigorously opposed to innovations. Only the brutal rupture of the
traditional 'establishment' could enable China to enter on a
period of change. Thus its progress has been made with less
resilience, speed and efficiency than in the case of Japan. In
order to throw overboard its old social and political ideology,
that a literate bureaucracy identified with the preservation of
things past, China had to adopt a social and political ideology
that permitted technological change; this has been the role of
communism in the recent history of the country. Japan, however, having avoided a sociopolitical revolution, has undergone a
much more rapid and profound technological revolution.

Vietnam, Korea and Taiwan were unable, under a colonial
regime, to undergo a technological revolution, for the colonial
powers did not wish for such a development. Since the attain-
ment of independence the potential accumulated through
Chinese civilisation has expressed itself in different ways: in
North Korea, under a communist regime; in South Korea, under
a capitalist regime that has had considerable industrial success in
a short space of time; in Taiwan, where also much technological
progress has been made under a capitalist regime. Hong Kong
gives a good idea of what Chinese industrial enterprise can
achieve. Only North Vietnam is still in too difficult a situation
for any real judgment to be made; but here, as in China, it would
appear that the complete breakdown of the old framework has
set in motion a technological revival.

CHAPTER 4

THE DENSITY OF POPULATION

All of the animal is in man, but not all of man is in the animal.

Chinese proverb

People are everywhere in the rural landscape. At all times of the year there are peasants working in the fields, bowing under their yokes along the straight, narrow footpaths, or fishing with rod and line on the edge of their flooded ricefields. In the muddy waters of the canals, square fishing nets are immersed and tirelessly hauled out. Now there will be a burial, with fifes and cymbals; the son of the dead man, dressed in sackcloth, walks backwards before the coffin; now a procession, with flags waving in the breeze, and the shrine of the guardian spirit carried by the faithful, a splash of red and gold amid the green of the ricefields. Every person is a spot of colour — the blue clothes of the Chinese, the brown of the Vietnamese, the white and blue of the Japanese. People are even present on the rivers, moving in sampans or actually grouped in floating villages (Fig. 14.24).

A thousand years of human occupation has obliterated the natural landscape of the plains: not a tree that has not been planted; not a pond that is not the result of excavation. The dykes, the only visible relief, have been raised at the cost of infinite labour; the earth that builds them has been excavated, transported and shaped by human labour only, without any mechanical assistance. There is not a square inch of ground that has not been turned and turned again by the hand of man for a thousand years or more; the fields have yielded two harvests a year, without interruption, for ten or twenty centuries. More than any other community in the world, the peasantry of the Far East, because of its stability over the centuries, and because of the respect paid to the dead, is really composed of more corpses than living beings. The cemeteries are pockmarked with graves, and even in the fields there are tiny mounds, avoided by the cultivators. Millions of dead bodies have rotted in this earth, for so long overpopulated; the dust and the alluvium are charged with impalpable human remains.

Such were the results of the 'peopling' quality, so essential a part of Far Eastern civilisation, that has put at the disposal of modern technology such vast masses of peasantry. Only the plains offered the right conditions; mountains and even hilly areas are but thinly peopled. A great contrast became established between the plains and their framework, a contrast between over-populated plains and deserted mountains. It is a contrast that is less apparent in Europe, where the mountains have more people (dependent on productive pastures) and the plains less (because of a more extensive agriculture). Frequently the people of the East Asiatic mountain regions are themselves different from those of the plains; nowhere is the contrast more marked than in northern Vietnam, where the mountain people, clothed in blue, are not of the same racial stock as the Vietnamians, whose clothes are brown. In China, despite the standardisation of cloth-ing colour, there is a very marked difference, over the whole of the southwestern region, between the mountain-dwellers and the inhabitants of the plains. The relations between highlands and lowlands are not the same as in the Western world, where the mountains send forth their streams of seasonal and permanent migrants. It is of no use in the Far Eastern mountains to look for exploiters of mountain products, or for religious foundations, or for animal showmen, or for chimney-sweeps (in any case Far Eastern houses have no chimneys). The few who dwell in the mountains keep to themselves; if the Miao, for example, emigrate anywhere it is really to colonise other mountains. At the present time the mountain peoples fear the encroachment of the plains-men, who take over the best lands and push them into the higher and less hospitable parts; this is actually happening in eastern Tibet and in the mountains of Annam (Figs. 3.1 and 4.3).

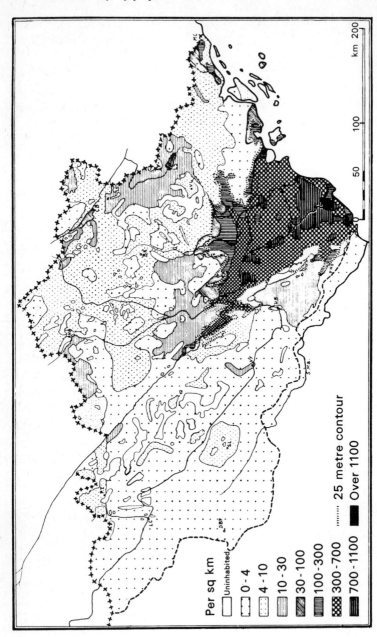

Per sq km

Uninhabited

0 - 4

4 - 10

10 - 30

30 - 100

100 - 300

300 - 700

700 - 1100

Over 1100

········· 25 metre contour

Fig. 4.1   Density of population in Tonkin in 1936. The map shows clearly the sharp contrast between the Red River delta and the surrounding mountains. The contrast corresponds roughly with the 25 m contour

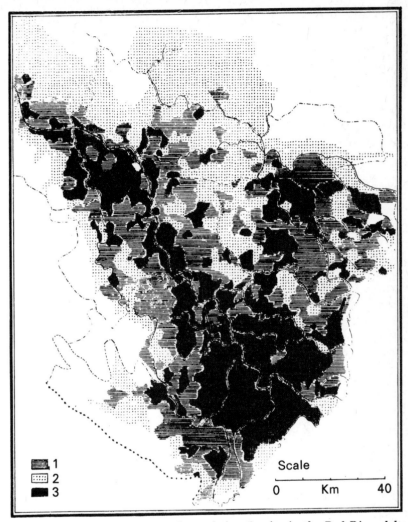

Fig. 4.2 Diagrammatic map of population density in the Red River delta in 1931. The non-deltaic areas are left blank (see Fig. 4.1).
Key: 1. average density (400−600 per km²); 2. lower than average density (between 100 and 400); 3. above average (over 600 per km²)

THE DELTA OF THE RED RIVER

This is a perfect example of a Far Eastern plain carefully exploited by a swarm of humanity. In 1931 its 15 000 km² carried

6.5 million rural dwellers, an average of 430 per km² of the whole area. Despite the recent political upheavals that have hindered population growth, and despite the lack of precise information, it can be conjectured with some confidence that the rural population approached 10 million by 1970, giving a density of 650 per km² (Figs. 4.1 and 4.2).

The population is a peasantry; the country it occupies is a rural landscape. Outside the towns (with which we are not immediately concerned) there are no industrial buildings, no factory chimneys. The population density equals or surpasses that of the most densely peopled industrial areas of Europe, and depends not on industry but on intensive agriculture and low consumption. In Europe, even a rural density of 100 per km² is rarely attained, but this figure is surpassed in every corner of the Red River delta.

The high density of population is a result of the civilisation and is not an inevitable consequence of the natural conditions. A whole complex structure of intensive agricultural techniques and an organisational framework of land management have been necessary to support such masses of humanity. The exploitation of the land has demanded a system of dykes (Fig. 7.2) to protect the fields from the ravages of the Red River, whose irregular and sometimes violent floods would otherwise completely inhibit agriculture over the greater part of the delta. However, the natural endowment must not be forgotten; the highest rural densities are found on the most fertile areas, which at the same time have the best hydraulic conditions — such as the parts of Nam Dinh and Thai Binh that lie along the river and its distributaries. Any geographical analysis, while emphasising the importance of the cultural factors, must at the same time underline the importance of the natural environment.

The surrounding mountains and hills are but lightly peopled; only a few hundred metres from the low and densely populated alluvial plains, one can enter the mountain solitudes. The average population density of the mountain areas of North Vietnam is only a dozen per square kilometre, and even this figure falls to four if the small but populated intermontane plains are omitted. There is not only a contrast of density, but also of people. The Vietnamians give way to Thay, Man and Miao. The Vietnam

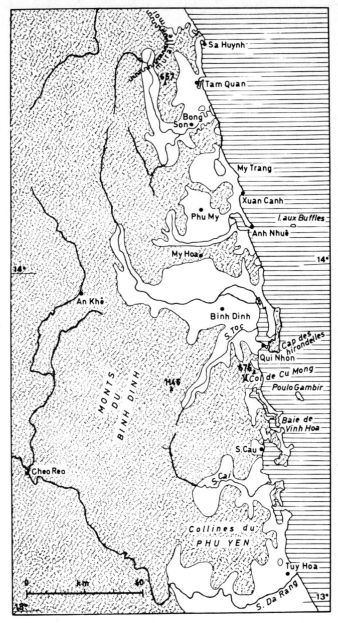

Fig. 4.3   Contrast between plains and mountains in Annam. The plains are densely peopled (by Vietnamese), the mountains are sparsely peopled (by Indonesians)

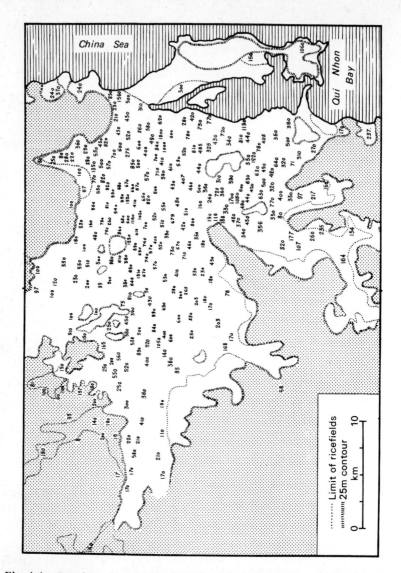

Fig. 4.4   Density of population in the plain of Binh Dinh, in Vietnam. The figures show the density per km^2 for each commune. Very sharp contrast between the plain, peopled by Vietnamians, and the surrounding hills, where, with the density falling almost to zero, the first representatives of the Indonesian peoples of the interior appear. The 25 m contour is sometimes separated from the high densities of the Vietnamian population by unoccupied terraces where ricefields could not be established. This was the situation in 1936. The Vietnamians took the place of the Cham in this plain in the fifteenth century

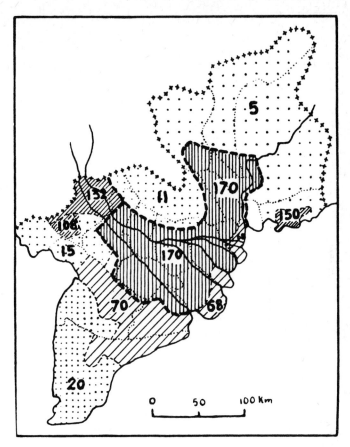

Fig. 4.5 Density of population in Cochinchina in 1936

peasants are loth to move into the hilly areas, where their health deteriorates rapidly; they talk of hostile spirits whom they attempt to placate by offering sacrifices on altars built at the junction of mountain and plain (Figs. 4.3 and 4.4).

It only needs one glance at these Vietnamians, returning from the mountains, anaemic, thin and pale, to see that they are victims of malaria. The hostile spirits of the mountains are indeed anopheles mosquitoes. Malaria is endemic in the uplands but is virtually absent from the Red River plain — a somewhat paradoxical situation since the plain has abundant surface water.

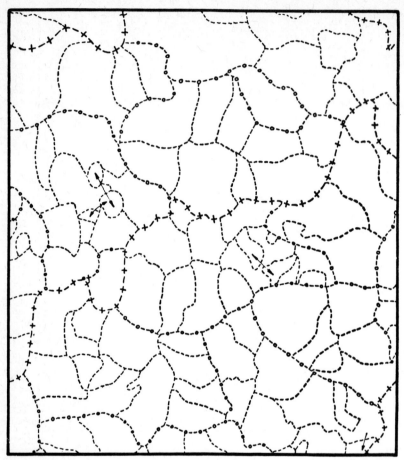

Fig. 4.6   **Administrative boundaries in the province of Bac Ninh, in the Red River delta. The communal areas are tiny, and their boundaries often sinuous; some communes are split (and the arrows show how the pieces join). Scale 1/100 000**

Nevertheless, the facts are clear enough; in only a few hundred metres one passes from the non-malarial delta to the very un-healthy foothills; the peasants are well aware of this, and much prefer to return to their plains villages to sleep rather than pass the night in the plantations where they are employed.

Mosquitoes of all kinds abound in the delta, from common gnats to tiny *Aedes*; the latter were responsible in 1969 for a

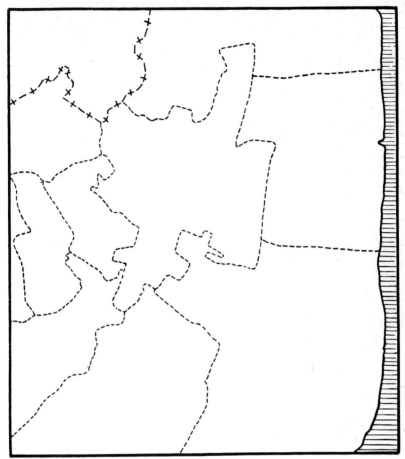

Fig. 4.7   Administrative boundaries in the province of Go Cong, in the Mekong delta. These are commune boundaries (and the scale is the same as Fig. 4.6. 1/100 000). The larger sizes are the result of younger age: these communes date from the nineteenth century, those of Bac Ninh are 1000 years old

terrible epidemic of dengue fever — terrible because it took on a haemorrhagic form that was frequently fatal, and because the *Aedes* were present in exceptional swarms. The genus *Anopheles* is widespread in the delta, but the prevalent species do not attack man and so do not transmit malaria. The larvae of the dangerous species do not like stagnant water, or muddy water in the shade, heavily laden with organic matter and full of larvae-eating fish. On the contrary, the larvae of the dangerous *Anopheles minimus* prefer the clear, fast-flowing, sun-bathed streams of the bordering hills. It is remarkable that the only parts of the delta where outbreaks of malaria have been noticed are along the seashore. Here, close to the river banks, the mixture of fresh water and sea spray gives the shallow ponds the exact degree of salinity demanded by the larvae of *Anopheles ludlowi* (*Sundaicus*); the sea breeze blows these mosquitoes some distance inland, where they attack human beings and transmit the *Plasmodium* that causes malaria.

The absence of malaria from the greater part of the delta is not a natural phenomenon; it results from the complete human occupation of the land. In its natural state the delta would have running streams exposed to sunlight; the dyking of the rivers, and the management of a continuous system of flooded ricefields created new conditions that were hostile to the *Anopheles* mosquito and favourable to man. Without knowing it, the people created an environment that fostered their own multiplication. But at the same time the Vietnamians, not having acquired any resistance to malarial infection, succumb much more quickly than the hill-peoples if they move outside their plains; the latter have developed a sort of immunity. So the delta peasant is right to want to avoid the mountains, and Vietnamese expansion was towards the south, from one plain to another, for 1200 kilometres to Cape Cambodia.

Such was the situation in 1940. Since then the discovery of antimalarial drugs and insecticides has completely upset the relation between man and the natural environment. Provided that the correct antimalarial and anti-*anopheles* techniques are observed, the delta peasant can now easily colonise the sparsely peopled areas of the mountains. Here is a geographical revolution. But colonisation – for what purpose? Not for wet rice, but for commercial products, the most important of which is tea.

The unhealthy malarial character of the mountain areas of North Vietnam was not the only reason for their sparsity of population and for the repugnance with which they were regarded by the peasants of the delta. There was another reason; wet rice cultivation, the speciality of the Vietnamese peasants, has only limited possibilities in the mountains; within the moun-

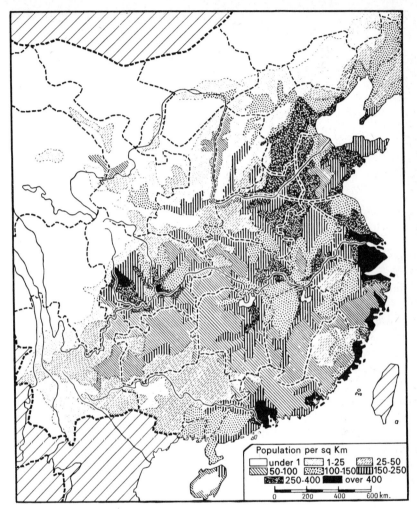

Fig. 4.8   Density of population in China, 1940

tain area of the former Tonkin province only 5 per cent of the
surface was occupied by ricefields. Since this tiny area did not
satisfy the mountain people, they practised forest clearance, and
the areas effectively harvested added another 5 per cent. In all
only 10 per cent of the total land surface was used for food
production — and that, bearing in mind also the poor yields, did

not permit the great density of population and the high degree of land management organisation that characterised the Vietnamian civilisation. Intensive manual agriculture found its general application only on the plain, and the contrast between the population densities in the plains and in the mountains was thus very sharp indeed.

The mountain peoples were much less numerous per square kilometre; but although they put less hard work into their cultivation than the plains peasants, they were no poorer. They fed just as well, and sold cattle, wood, fruit and roots from the forest, and mushrooms. Certain valleys even had an air of rural prosperity, with large houses (Figs. 14.7 and 14.8) scattered among bamboo thickets, women leisurely spinning and weaving, casting an occasional glance at the rice-hulling hammer worked by a flowing stream (Fig. 7.6). This machine symbolises the prosperity of the mountain peoples as against the poverty of the plains, for the delta peasant spends long hours husking rice in a hand-worked mill and then polishing it with a pedal-worked hammer that falls into a mortar. The mountain-dweller uses water power; the hammer is activated by a paddle wheel, or by the alternate filling and emptying of a ladle on the end of a lever. The birds fly round the mortar, swooping down to peck when the lever is up, and flying off the moment it falls.

CHINA

The traditional China has bequeathed to modern China a population map of the same kind, but enormously amplified. Though the delta of the Si-Kiang is of similar dimensions to that of the Red River, and though the plains of Kwangtung, Fukien and southern Chekiang are small (albeit numerous), central and northern China present immense alluvial expanses (Fig. 4.8). In central China there are the valley of the Blue River, with its extensions in the lake-filled depressions of Tung ting (the Siang River) and Po yang (the Kan River), in the Han valley, and especially the vast delta of the Yangtse. The plain of the lower Hwai provides a link between central and northern China. In north China the immense plain, covering 400 000 km², is prolonged almost without interruption into the vastness of Man-

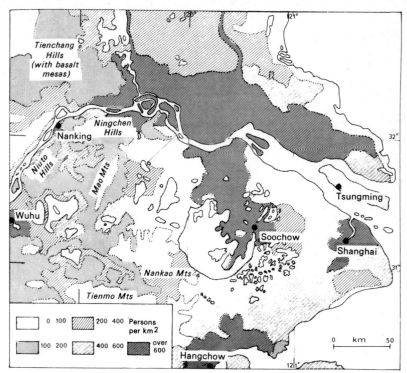

Fig. 4.9   Density of population in the lower Yangtse area (after H. von Wissmann, 'Südwest-Kiangsu, der Wuhu-Taihu Kanal und das Problem des Yangtse-Deltas', *Wissenschaftliche Veroffentlichungen des Deutschen. Museums für Länderkunde zu Leipzig*, N.F.8, 1940, 63–106)

churia, which nearly reaches the basins of the Liao and Sungari rivers. Attached to it are the plains of the Wei and Fen valleys; and northern China includes also immense loess plateaux in Shensi, Shansi and Kansu. In the plains of southern and central China the rural population density is always high, and sometimes very high indeed; some parts of the Si Kiang delta have more than 1000 rural inhabitants per km², and it is the same in the Yangtse delta (e.g., the island of Tsong Ming), in the several small littoral plains of Fukien and Chekiang and in the plain of Chengtu (Szechwan) (Figs. 4.9 and 4.10).

The contrast between mountain and plain remains very striking, even though the climate renders the mountain areas

Fig. 4.10   Relief of the lower Yangtse area (after H. von Wissmann, 'Zur Karte von Mittelchina', *Zeitschrift für Geopolitik*, 12, 1938, 942–4). The altitudes are approximate

healthier than those of Indochina. But Chinese agricultural techniques were developed for the plains, and do not give such
rewards for effort in the mountains. Often the mountains and
hills, having been denuded of their forests, bear no more than a
poor, bush-studded herbage, and are of no economic value. However there are some exceptions: thanks to their tea plantations,
the mountains of Chekiang and Fukien have between 50 and 100
persons per km^2; and the Red Basin of Szechwan is the most
charming mountain area in all China, with a scattering of isolated
houses in among the carefully tilled fields, set in an environment
of pine-clad sandstone hills.

JAPAN

As long ago as the mid-1930s the demographic evolution of
Japan was sufficiently far advanced for there to be no longer a
majority of peasants in the population. This trend has continued;
the Japanese countryside continues to be densely peopled, but
the excess population has moved to the towns, and though the
number of peasant cultivators has not yet begun to diminish,
their proportion of the total population has declined very
rapidly. The rural population density results from a certain type
of civilisation; and though this was rather different from that of
China in its techniques of land management, it was just as effective in enabling vast numbers of people to live and multiply on
the land (Fig. 4.11).

Thanks to latitude, the demographic contrast between mountain and plain cannot be explained by differences in the healthi-
ness of the environment; rather it is due to steep slopes and poor
soils that do not lend themselves to cultivation. Further,
Japanese farming techniques do not extend to the exploitation of
mountain pastures, so there are no 'alps', no milk, butter or
cheese. One mountain near Kyoto has acquired a reputation for
the production of excellent cheese — but it is made from soya
beans! Japanese peasants have not lost the art of cultivating
forest clearings in areas of lesser slope, and the alternation of
short periods of cultivation and long forest fallows still occurs,
despite the opposition of the forestry interests. In Shikoku the

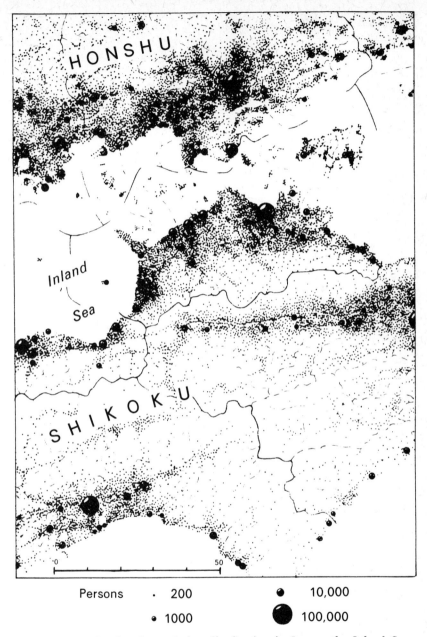

Persons · 200 ● 10,000
● 1000 ● 100,000

Fig. 4.11   A sample of population distribution in Japan: the Inland Sea
(from 1/1M map of the 1960 census, published in 1963 by Bureau of
Statistics, Tokyo). The map shows clearly the influence of the mountains

paper-mulberry is cultivated in this way, and its bark is used for making banknote paper.

Japanese energy, unhindered by any liability to malaria, has exploited the hills, the terraces and gentler slopes, even though their fertility may be poor, by the construction of narrow terraces for the growing of tea, mulberry and vegetables. In those areas that are completely cultivated, plains and hills alike, the population density decreases from south to north; it is very high on the best lands of Kyushu, on the margins of the Inland Sea, in the environs of Kyoto and Tokyo, and lower on the plains of the west coast of Honshu and on those of Hokkaido. The increasingly cool climate towards the north rules out the possibility of two harvests a year.

HIGH DENSITIES

Far Eastern civilisation has established relations between cultivated land and the peasantry that demand high rural population densities. Whether in North Vietnam, in China, Korea or Japan, the number of peasants per km² of cultivated land is extremely high, rarely less than 300, and often over 1000, with maxima of about 1600. Such maxima are attained in the canton of Tra Lu (in the Red River delta), in certain cantons of the Si Kiang delta, in the small plains of Fukien and Chekiang, in the delta of the Yangtse, and in the plains of southern Japan. This means that on each cultivated hectare, some parts of the Far East have more than ten peasants (men, women and children) deriving their sustenance and even selling a small part of their harvest to pay their taxes and to buy, in tiny quantities, such things as they do not themselves produce but regard as indispensable. 'Land and man in the Far East' implies a certain kind of relation between man and the land. It is the product of a certain quality of civilisation, giving rise to a peculiar and characteristic geographical landscape, difficult to understand unless its origins are recognised.

These very high population densities over wide areas in the Far East are proof of an advanced civilisation, for a degree of technological, social and political development is indispensable in the solution of their problems. Groups of people with less advanced technology are likely to have less close relations with each other, and to remain at a fairly low density. The very high densities of the Far East, on the other hand, require good village administration within a strong legal framework, irrigation, flood control, a system of justice and of taxation, defence against external dangers, an educational system, censuses and maps. All this implies highly organised and efficient states, with good media for transport and trade so that complementary regions may exchange their products. Such states inevitably imply the existence of cities, centres of administration and commerce, and of diverse secondary activities. The Far Eastern peoples have tackled the modern technological age with large manpower resources because they have been in an advanced stage of civilisation for a long time. The peasants have responded to the growth of population by increasing their crop yields and diversifying their techniques. 'Civilisation', says Grenier[1], 'consists of a constant effort to raise resources to the level of needs.'

DEMOGRAPHIC GROWTH

The Far Eastern peoples have need of refined and progressive techniques to cope with a demographic growth that has accelerated since the reduction of the death rate by improved health services.

Traditionally the female peasants were very fertile; they married young, usually under the age of twenty, and procreated until the menopause; unless their fertility was hindered by impaired health, they would produce a child every year for more than twenty years. Feminine fecundity and a large family were highly appreciated; sterile men and women were scorned. Contraceptive practices were not unknown; Chinese pharmacies had for long sold abortive drugs, but without any noticeable resulting fall in the birth rate. The peasants desired a large family, so as to guarantee the continuance of ancestor worship; but this cult of ancestors was not a prerequisite for the proliferation, for the Catholic peasants of Vietnam and China had just as large families as their non-Christian brothers. There were no celibates, and a

[1] M. A. Grenier, *Annales d'Histoire économique et sociale*, 1930, p. 30.

very high marriage rate. In China there were 120 newlyweds per annum per 10 000 population, as against 85 in France. Marriage posed fewer problems than in Western countries, for when a son married, his wife and children were supported by the father as head of the family.

With the birth rate remaining at a high level after the introduction of modern hygiene, a population explosion followed, particularly in Japan, where traditionally there had been some control over the birth rate (that was abolished about 1868), and where modern medicine penetrated with great rapidity. Previously, a very high death rate had been compensated by great fertility; in China, for example, at least twenty children out of every hundred born alive died within twelve months, and many mothers and children died of tetanus, a result of umbilical cords being cut with a bit of old pottery or a bamboo leaf. Smallpox sometimes decimated the entire child population of a village, although the Chinese had discovered an empirical method of vaccination. Other epidemics, fostered by famines, carried off multitudes of peasants. All the endemic diseases of the Old World were well established, and the spread of intestinal parasites was furthered by the use of human excreta as fertiliser.

In the 1930s the population of China was very young, indicative of very high birth and death rates; few individuals attained old age, and of 1000 Chinese, only forty-two were over the age of sixty, compared with 125 in France. Old people were thus held in high esteem because of their rarity; longevity was a sign of good fortune, and a family or a village blessed with numerous aged persons was regarded as specially favoured by nature.

During the course of centuries and millennia, mortality naturally swallowed up the products of such abundant fecundity. Nevertheless the Far Eastern countries reached the modern era not with a few dozen millions of people, but with hundreds or thousands of millions. It is worth reminding ourselves that even a growth rate of 1 per cent per annum will cause the population to double in seventy years, and that a birth rate of 4 per cent and a death rate of 3 per cent (which is enormous) ensures this 1 per cent growth — so that a population of 1000 persons in the year 1000 BC would have grown to 4 million million by 1940. Mortality has of course been the principal brake, but it was aided by infanticide, practised (especially on girl babies) by the Chinese and Japanese.

The Chinese population grew slowly through the centuries, in a saw-toothed curve that reflects alternating periods of growth and regression. Long ago, Chinese political philosophers were pointing out the disadvantages of overpopulation. Thus Mencius wrote, 'a population that continues to grow for a long period will fall in disarray'; and Han Fei Tseu:

> Hitherto, the population was small, but prosperous and peaceful; the government neither rewarded nor punished them, for they knew how to behave. Nowadays, it appears that five sons are not enough; each son has five sons of his own, and the grandfather, before he dies, thus has twenty-five descendants. The population, more numerous and less prosperous, works hard to gain but little. Even if the authorities punished and rewarded twice as much, the disorders could not be prevented.

The same author also wrote:

> During a spring famine, an elder brother takes part of his younger brother's rations; this is not the result of lack of fraternal affection, but simply of poverty. If the autumn harvest is good, food will be given away to passers-by. The alleged generosity of a previous age thus signifies nothing, it was just a symptom of greater prosperity; our present troubles are due to a reduction in the standard of life.

These thoughts came from the fourth and third centuries BC; true, they are somewhat coloured by their reference to a mythical golden age when everything was much better than at the time of writing.

The demographic situation is being rapidly transformed at the present time, with Japan offering the most interesting and varied changes. The revolution of 1868 had the effect of lifting the restriction of births and at the same time lowering the death rate. So the population increased very rapidly, from 30 million in 1868 to 84 million in 1952. But then the Japanese nation, on the advice of its leaders, decided to reduce its birth rate, either by contraceptive devices or by abortions, in order to prevent too rapid a growth. In Taiwan, the birth rate has been much reduced by the liberal use of contraceptive pills. In China it has been reduced by later marriages, by the frequent separation of husbands and wives, and by birth control devices (though the eating of tadpoles by women was an unsuccessful one of these). Despite all these happenings the potential demographic growth of the Far Eastern peasantry, conditioned by their huge numbers and their continued high birth rate, remains enormous.

CHAPTER 5

AN AGRICULTURAL CIVILISATION

Literature and agriculture are the two primary
professions. All mechanical arts have something evil
about them; the study of literature is the only noble
activity.

Chinese proverb

The occupations of the elite are not those of the
poor. Amongst the former, intellectual pursuits, and
the latter, physical labour. The intellectuals govern
the rest, and are supported by them.

Mencius (372–288 BC)

The traditional Chinese civilisation was above all agricultural and
rural. True, a brilliant court surrounded the 'Son of Heaven' and
a refined mandarin society shed lustre on the great cities such as
Su Chow and Hangchow. But at least nine-tenths of the population lived on the cultivated fields.

The high importance attached to agriculture was recognised in
the official philosophy, which accorded second ranking to cultivators, after the *literati* but above artisans and merchants. It was
the same in Japan, except that the nobility took the place of the
literati. One of the important functions of the Emperor (the 'Son
of Heaven') was the performance of the agrarian rites by which
he assured good harvests for his people. Common themes in
Chinese literature exalted the beauty and nobility of the cultivator's life; many scholars, in their declining years, retired to
their native village, there to renew contact with the peasants,

who regarded them with great respect. They started, or continued, to write poems in praise of things rural; their poems described in elegant language the humdrum labours of seedtime and harvest. Such Georgics had a flavour of good literature, and were intended less as examples of rustic poetry than as demonstrations of the erudition of their author and his skill in selecting passages from earlier works to compose a harmonious literary patchwork. No scholar ever returned to the land or handled a plough, even if he had not had an administrative career; a scholar rejected by the society of mandarins would never consent to wield a hoe, and would prefer the life of a low-ranking scribe in the *yamen* of a sub-prefect or in a village school.

However, the idea of rural simplicity exalted by the lettered class certainly had its influence on the evolution of China; it was not in vain that poets and philosophers, through the centuries, extolled the attractions of country life, asserting that the basis of family happiness and prosperity lay firmly rooted in the soil. One person of high rank, who became generalissimo and prime minister, pointed out that in order to prosper a family should respect four principles: to feed the fish in the pond, to raise pigs, to plant bamboos and to cultivate vegetables. Confucianism and Taoism, each in its own way, also glorified the same rustic ideal, the former in praising the virtuous simplicity of rural life, the latter in preaching the return to nature and the communion of human beings and inanimate objects.

The effects of these rural prejudices were considerable, for they engendered in the lettered classes a real hostility towards the possible political pretentions of the urban population. From the Emperor himself to the last of the peasants the wind of politics could only blow via the single channel of the mandarin hierarchy. There were no intermediate autonomous organisations, and no urban franchise. The opposition, the agitation and the political evolution that the towns might have provided was completely lacking in China, a fact that was not without importance when the country came to re-orient itself politically.

A mandarinate dreaming of a rural life was inevitably very conservative; it could not imagine that China could and would be subject to profound transformations. It was incapable of taking the revolutionary decisions made by some Japanese aristocrats,

helped by a powerful merchant class. And finally, o.
the glorification of rural good fortune did much to
large population on the fields, causing that extreme \ ..y
that created its own peculiar problems in the transformation of
China.

INTENSIVE AGRICULTURE

The very high population densities were dependent on the intensive techniques of agriculture; on the other hand these traditional
techniques were ill-adapted to the extensive cultivation of large
areas. In other words, a small number of Chinese peasants spread
over large areas would have cultivated only a small proportion of
the surface; the density over the whole area would be small, but
the density on the cultivated area would be high.

Urged on by necessity and by traditional routine, the peasant
works very hard to ensure his family's livelihood and earn sufficient money for purchases and taxes. He is not at pains to relate
his labour to his income. If the budget of a small Far Eastern
agricultural holding were drawn up so as to pay the proprietor a
labourer's wage, it would invariably be in the red. To remain
within the realm of reality in the Far East one must discount
peasant labour, and only take into account expenses corresponding to the consumption of home-produced goods; in effect, a
payment in kind.

The smaller the holdings and the denser the peasant population, the more labour appears to be necessary. The peasants of
the Red River delta expend enormous effort in the cultivation of
their tiny ricefields, from which they may obtain two or three
harvests in twelve months. In the Mekong delta, with a sparser
population and less intensive techniques, only one harvest a year
is reaped (Figs. 5.1 and 5.2). It is the same in Japan: in the
northern isle of Hokkaido, which is the least peopled of the
Japanese islands, the production in 1927 was valued at 184 yen
per hectare, employing 0.54 persons, whereas in Kagawa, the
most densely peopled part of Honshu, production was 881 yen
per hectare, employing 3.89 persons. Japan had developed sericulture to help its rural population, and whilst rice cultivation

required 250 man-days per hectare, sericulture required 500 man-days.

Far Eastern agriculture did not entirely neglect the use of draught animals. Oxen and horses were used in Japan, oxen in Korea and in northern China, oxen and buffaloes in the Yangtse valley and in south China and in Vietnam. But it made little use of animals in ploughing, for reasons that will become apparent later on. Machines were unknown, and the amount of human labour employed on one hectare was enormously greater than in a mechanised agricultural system. One hectare of wheat in China required 600 hours of human labour, but only twenty-six hours in the United States. For one hour of labour, the Chinese peasant produced 1.1 kg of maize (45.5 kg in the United States), or 1.6 kg of wheat (39.4 kg in the United States). In the Red River delta in 1935, taking account of all the labour involved in producing and husking 1 kg of husked rice required three hours of human effort. However, the labour required from each peasant is not excessive; even if the land is intensely cultivated, a peasant is only employed full time for 180 days in a year.

Far Eastern agriculture is indeed intensive; this is its major characteristic. But the intensity of agricultural labour has not the same significance in the traditional Far East and under modern technological conditions. In the latter, intensive agriculture obtains the maximum yield per hectare by using genetically selected seed and carefully calculated quantities of balanced fertilisers, together with pesticides produced by the synthetic chemical industry, and the employment of a minimum of man-power with a maximum use of motorised machinery. The high cost of labour means that intensification is only possible through mechanisation. If the enterprise is not proving profitable its expenses must be reduced by becoming less intensive, or even reverting to extensive if this is the only way of making a profit.

The traditional intensive agriculture of the Far East was very different; it used technical wisdom, it is true, but this was empirical and not scientific. It employed large quantities of manures, but only of the organic variety, chemical fertilisers being quite unknown. The struggle against insect pests was an entirely manual one. No machines of any kind were employed, only a liberal supply of human labour. There was no accounting system, nor any idea of making a profit; all that mattered was to keep the peasants alive. Intensive labour was an absolute necessity. True, as we have seen, there was some interdependence of population density and agricultural techniques; but once this interdependence was established, the peasant could not get out of intensive labour without dying of hunger.

SMALL FIELDS

The plains are cultivated with meticulous care; not an inch of cultivable land escapes the hoe. As this kind of cultivation is inappropriate for sloping land with poorer soils, the cultivated areas of the Far East cover but a small proportion of the whole surface — only 27 per cent in China (traditional China of the 'eighteen provinces', excluding Manchuria and the western extensions) and 15 per cent in Japan. Compare these figures with Western Europe, where France, for example, has 65 per cent of its surface under crops and grass, and England 68 per cent.

The smallness of the cultivated fields is aggravated by partition resulting from inheritance, which leads to an extreme fragmentation with plots of garden size. It would be inappropriate to call it horticulture, for the tiny plots are ploughed to produce cereals, not vegetables or fruit. The marked preference for wet rice cultivation leads to the parcelling, not of properties but of the actual cultivated areas, for the moment there is the slightest slope, terraces and bunds must be constructed to retain the rainwater which is the principal means of irrigation; the size of the embanked compartments diminishes as the slope increases.

This fragmentation has not the troublesome consequences in the Far East that it has in Europe. In the absence of heavy implements, the small size of the plots does not hinder the operations. Since the plough and the harrow omit the corners of fields, the careful peasant returns with a hoe; the more corners, the more work for the hoe. But this is not an undue burden on the peasant, who, after all, does not have far to go from the village to his fields, which are seldom distant. A greater hindrance is the need to maintain the bunds between paddyfields, for these sensibly reduce the cultivable area. It has been estimated in Japan

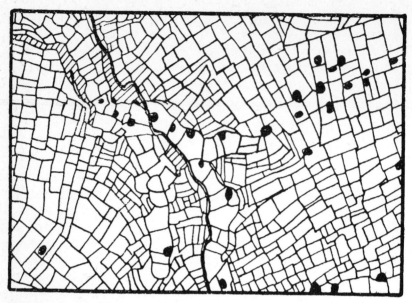

Fig. 5.1   **Fragmentation of cultivated land in the Red River delta. This is
an extreme example of tiny fields; not a scrap of land is uncultivated, save
for the bunds between the ricefields, which are rectangular in shape. The
small black areas are ponds. Scale 1/10 000**

that a rational reorganisation of the ricefields might increase the
harvest by 15 per cent, through the gain in cultivated area and
the better control of drainage and irrigation. The bunds separ-
ating paddyfields often give rise to disputes and conflicts, for
unscrupulous owners may pare the bunds to their own advantage,
or even displace them to the detriment of their neighbours. The
peasants like the division of their holdings into separate parcels,
for this enables them to take advantage of the different qualities
of each parcel and to vary and to stagger the harvests from each
one, thus reducing the risk of crop failure and helping to spread
the work over the year.

On the areas of dry cultivation and moderate population
density in northern China the average size of holdings was 0.45
hectares; on the low rice-growing plains of the lower Yangtse it
was 0.30 ha, with frequent examples of less than 0.05 ha. More
than half the irrigated paddyfields in Japan were under 500
square metres in size, and the fragmentation had proceeded

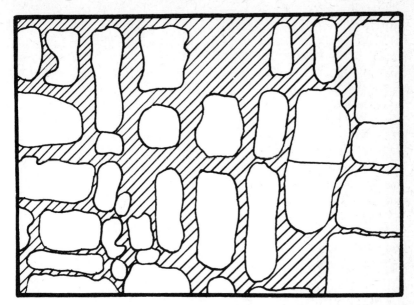

Fig. 5.2 Fragmentation of cultivated land in Cambodia. Same scale (1/10 000) as Fig. 5.1. Large ricefields with rounded outlines, convenient for ploughing. The shaded portions bear only sugar palms (*Borassus*) and are little used

much further in Japan than in China. In the Red River delta a holding of one hectare was on average divided into six parcels; in some villages the greater part of the surface was divided into parcels of under 500 or even 300 square metres. A comparison with the Mekong delta is revealing, for in 1935 a single province of 1000 km² in the Tonkin delta contained more parcels than the whole of 'Cochinchina' with its 65 000 km² (Figs. 5.1 and 5.2).

Before the agrarian revolutions that followed the Second World War, the Far East was one vast area of minute landholdings. The small properties were indeed infinitesimal, and even the large ones would have surprised a small French farmer by their exiguity. Although many peasants were in fact proprietors, their private holdings were so restricted that only the modest nature of their demands enabled them to subsist. Before the agrarian reform of 1946, more than two-thirds of the peasant families of Japan cultivated areas of under one hectare; the area cultivated by an adult agricultural worker averaged 0.36 ha, whereas in the

United States the comparable figure was 12.8 ha, in Denmark 6.4, in France 2.4 and in Italy 1.2 ha. Five million Japanese owned a total of 6.2 million ha; of these, 2.5 million held less than 0.5 ha, 1.2 million between 0.5 and 1 ha, and 900 000 between 1 and 3 ha. A 'large farm' was over 3 ha in size. But large holdings did not mean large-scale farming, for these Japanese 'latifundia' were let out in tenant farms of very small size. The agrarian reform of 1946 redistributed the land, and the tenants became proprietors; but still, after the reform as before it, the adult Japanese peasant cultivated only an average of 0.36 ha. However, he now had no rent to pay, and the price that he had to pay for the purchase of the land did not ruin him.

In Korea, in 1938, some 3 300 000 landholders cultivated a total of 4.3 million ha; the size of the average holding was thus a little over one hectare, but each adult peasant cultivated only 0.25 ha. The lot of the Korean peasant was aggravated by the encroachment of Japanese colonists. Following the capitulation of August 1945, however, the Nipponese were repatriated and their lands confiscated. Thereafter, North Korea and South Korea have followed different paths.

The total cultivated area of China proper (i.e., excluding Manchuria, Mongolia and Tibet) was 85 million hectares in 1935, comprising about 55 million 'farms', the average size of which was thus about 1.5 ha. The holdings were larger, and the peasant proprietors relatively fewer, in northern China than in the centre and south. Sixty-five per cent of the peasants owned their land in the north, 30 per cent in Chekiang. Around the great cities of the Yangtse and southern China, 95 per cent of the farmers were tenants, for the traders and industrialists of the cities had invested part of their profits in land. The number of persons in each family was in direct relationship to the area cultivated: the smaller the farm, the smaller the family. While the average size of families owning less than 0.6 ha was four persons, families owning more than 5 ha numbered at least 7.3 persons. It is true that the difference results in part from the fact that a larger holding permitted more members of the family to remain at home, but we must not forget the direct effect of economic conditions on the survival of children and adults, for those in poverty succumbed more easily during famines.

In the Red River delta a cultivated area of 1.2 million hectares was divided between 950 000 farmers, giving an average size of 1.2 ha. Here again there was a predominance of very small holdings; those of under one hectare covered 600 000 ha, and 600 000 farmers had on an average under 0.36 ha. Holdings of medium size, between 1 and 3.6 ha, covered 400 000 ha; large properties of over 3.6 ha covered 200 000 ha. The 'medium' range represents a holding that was impossible for a single family to cultivate; either hired labour must be employed, or part of the land rented out. Sometimes such proprietors would do no cultivation themselves, but would direct the hired labour and busy themselves with administrative functions in the village. For however assiduous a cultivator the Vietnamese peasant might be, he still considered it honourable to abandon agriculture, and an aura of social prestige surrounded those who no longer worked on the land.

Laws and customs were both traditionally hostile towards large estates; the royal government periodically ordered their subdivision, while the peasants were united against those who attempted to acquire large properties. It was very difficult to buy land in a village if one was not a citizen of the place; the purchaser could well be swindled, and after being paid an agreed price find himself in direct confrontation with the rightful owner. The parochial authorities inflicted many harassments on a landowner who was not a native of the village, and the local inhabitants would refuse to work for him; in the last resort, the newcomer would be reduced to selling up and cutting his losses. These hindrances placed in the way of land purchase by outsiders had effectively prevented the creation of large estates.

The foregoing paragraphs make clear the exact nature of the relationship between man and the land in the traditional Far East. The cultivator was indeed a peasant, tied to the land by the desire to obtain some monetary reward and even more so by the necessity to produce his own food, by a feeling of solidarity with his neighbours, and by the emotions aroused in him by the thought that his ancestors were buried in the village or even under the very earth that he cultivated.

Despite the variety and uncertainty of the available statistics, it is possible to discern a degree of uniformity in the size of rural properties throughout the Far East: in Japan 1.24 ha, in Korea 1.13 ha, in the Red River delta 1 ha, and in China 1.5 ha. The average figure for China was somewhat higher than the others by reason of the inclusion of the more extensive farms of the dry northwest. The Vietnam figure was lowest because almost the whole of the cultivated area lay in the deltas; the Chinese deltas, taken alone, would have given equally low values.

It is not surprising that agricultural wage-earners were few in number. It is true that at the moment of maximum need, paid labour was sought in those regions that had a surplus, but all-the-year-round wages were rare indeed. The employees were very poorly paid, but were treated as members of the family, housed, clothed and fed by the employer. In many villages of northern Vietnam and in Korea, communal land, redistributed at regular intervals, served to provide the landless peasants with a few square metres to cultivate.

What possibilities were open to the peasant who had made a little money out of careful agriculture, or to the villager who had profited from trade, industry or administration, and wished to return to his native village in his old age to be near his ancestors? The first thing was usually to build a nice house for his descendants. Also he might buy land — a possibility in his own village but still difficult and expensive; one way of accomplishing it was to offer a loan on the security of part of the debtor's land; sales, subject to the right of the vendor to repurchase, were frequent. Such arrangements were convenient to peasants who were reluctant to surrender, without hope of recovery, their ancestral family land.

Bearing in mind what was said above about the obstacles put in the way of a 'foreign' buyer, it is clear that the price of land varied from village to village in accordance with supply and demand and not according to its fertility; in those villages where numerous people had enriched themselves through trade, land was very dear. In the Red River delta in 1938, and in the currency of the period, the price of a piece of fertile cultivable land varied between 3000 and 27 000 French francs per hectare. In northern China, the average value of one hectare of cultivated land in 1927 was 400 Chinese dollars, or about 5000 French francs; in the lower Yangtse it was 880 Chinese dollars, or 11 000

French francs. Studies at this time showed that the lowest price was 195 dollars, the highest 1725. There is nothing surprising about these prices, for they were lower than agricultural land prices in France at the same period — a good vineyard in Bas-Languedoc would have sold at 30 000 French francs per hectare. But the income of a Far Eastern peasant was only one-tenth that of a French peasant, so the purchase price of a piece of land was a sum that the Far Eastern peasant found it almost impossible to raise.

Small sums could be hoarded as cash. A peasant would hide some coins in a carefully concealed hole in his mudbrick wall, or under a flagstone. A wealthier person, possessing a greater hoard, would have more secret hiding places or might even immerse it at the bottom of a pond. But hoarded money yielded nothing and was by no means safe. It was difficult to keep wealth a secret. In the Chinese countryside the mandarin police were very slack, and bandits endeavoured to steal treasures the whereabouts of which had been indicated to them by members of secret societies that were widespread among the villages. Robberies were particularly numerous on the eve of the New Year festival.

CHAPTER 6

AGRICULTURAL TECHNIQUES

To pursue science and not love your fellow-men is to light a torch and close your eyes.

Chinese proverb

In order to understand Far Eastern agricultural methods, it is necessary constantly to bear in mind the differences between such methods and those of the Western world. In the West, farmers seek to obtain as high a profit as possible; if the results are not satisfactory, the methods may be changed, new cultivated crops may be substituted or the farmer may even turn from cultivation to stock-rearing which requires less labour. If agriculture becomes too unremunerative, the Western 'peasants' just leave the land and seek an easier existence through employment in industry, transport or commerce. For the Far Eastern peasant, the circumstances are very different; his immediate problem is to live on his land and to derive his sustenance from its produce; there is no escape from rural life. Any thoughts of costs, of the price of labour per cultivated hectare, are submerged by the threat of famine. In order to live, the Far Eastern peasant must produce food, whatever the cost in human labour.

SKILFUL EMPIRICISM

Once it is understood that Far Eastern agricultural techniques are not directed towards reducing the amount of manpower required, they appear skilful and sensible, albeit empirical and unscientific; their wisdom has indeed often anticipated modern discoveries in the physical chemistry of soils. Among the wise practices derived from agelong and patient observations are the fanatical use of every source of manure traditionally available to the peasantry, the judicious use of green manure, the making of composts that transform vegetable matter into humus, the 'invention' of tea, the discovery of sericulture, and the use of incubators.

In the eighteenth century Chinese and Japanese agriculture was superior in many respects to that of Europe; the Far Eastern peasants by their careful practice of manuring had done away with fallows, and so had appreciably increased the harvested area which indeed equalled the whole cultivable surface. Early visitors from Europe were much struck by the ingenuity of the Chinese peasants, and credited them with the most marvellous and complicated agricultural techniques. Here, for example, is what the Swedish navigator Charles-Gustav Ekeberg told the Royal Swedish Academy of Science in 1754: 'reliable Swedish sources', he said, told him that in the province of Fukien the people

> made rafts, covered them with straw matting, placed soil on them and planted rice in it with much profit; true, these floating fields were sometimes damaged by hurricanes, but they were regarded as very lucrative, because in times of drought as well as during the rains, the water underneath assured an even humidity, and heavy rain did not damage them because it quickly ran away. Here is a proof of their industry that is well worth considering.

This fable was still current even at the end of the nineteenth century, and a French geography text of that time was still writing that the ricefields of the Tonkin delta were on floating rafts.

A HAND LABOUR AGRICULTURE

Far Eastern agriculture used but few animals and even fewer machines. Its implements were ingenious, but simple and easy to make — from wood and bamboo. The Chinese knew how to construct waterwheels, driven by riverflow, that allowed them to irrigate lands at a higher level than the watercourse. Such wheels

Fig. 6.1   A noria worked by a stream (from an eighteenth-century Chinese drawing). The stream (in the foreground) activates the noria, and the bamboo tubes discharge their contents into a ditch (centre, right); in the background is a newly planted ricefield

were to be found as far south as Kwang Ngai, to the south of Tourane (Da Nang); it would appear that they were not a Chinese invention, but used a technique of Central Asian origin. The Chinese also knew how to build windmills, but different from those of the West in that they turned on a horizontal plane and not a vertical one. But these machines of wood, bamboo and sail-cloth were unimportant exceptions; Far Eastern agriculture was almost entirely dependent on human labour, even for such dreary and toilsome tasks as irrigation. The normal implements found on any farm would be a ladle for irrigation water, a spade, hoe, plough, harrow, sickle, machete, with yokes and panniers for carrying things. The whole lot, in 1935, would not have exceeded 200 French francs in value.

The plains were cultivated to the last square metre. Needy peasants — and weren't they all? — would even plant a row or two of rice on the river banks; it might get washed away by a flood, but they took a chance, and if it succeeded, there were a few extra handfuls of grain to be harvested.

In Japan, it has been estimated that a field of cucumbers yields eight times as much fruit as an American cultivator would get from the same area. Furthermore, the Japanese peasant grows his cucumbers on stakes, and can thus grow another crop in between the rows, whereas in the United States the plants creep over the ground and so occupy it completely. The Japanese gardener treats each plant as an individual and cares for it according to its needs; he often feeds it with human urine, more or less diluted according to the amount of rainfall. The apple-growers of Tsugaru, in the north of Honshu — an area that yields over half of all the apples in Japan — wrap each fruit in paper to protect it from insects and cryptogamic diseases; it is not a question of producing superlative fruit for a luxury market.

The practice of sericulture in the Far East demands a great deal of labour. The young silkworms require scrupulous atten-tion, and the older ones need great quantities of mulberry leaves, at inconvenient hours, so that the silkworm cultivator works day and night.

The Chinese provinces of Anhwei and Kiangsu grow winter wheat on land that is used for rice in summer. As the fields are badly drained the peasants build earthbanks, above the level of the floodable paddyfield, that remain dry and usable for wheat. After the wheat has been harvested the banks are demolished, and the field, flattened once more, can grow wet rice.

In the provinces of Nam Dinh and Thai Binh, in the delta of the Red River, the soil, after the November harvest and the drying-out of the paddyfield, is ploughed or broken up with a hoe; clods of earth are lifted by hand and piled up into little walls; the subsoil is then dug with a spade and each clod is turned over. The walls of topsoil clods are then dismantled and rebuilt so as to ensure complete drying-out; after six weeks they are finally dismantled and the clods are pulverised with a mallet; then the swing-plough levels the whole field off. This operation, which takes 150 days of labour per hectare, has beneficial effects; in a region with very deep alluvial soils, it allows the fertility of the lower layers to be utilised, aerates the soil, and increases crop yields by an estimated 40 per cent. A rice yield of 2000 kg per hectare may be converted into 2800 kg, but the extra 800 kg will have cost 150 days' labour. At the 1938 price of 50 French francs per 100 kg of rice, the payment for one day's labour would have been a mere 2.60 francs. And of course, the advantage of the whole operation might be lost if the clod walls collapse through heavy winter rain.

The Tonkin peasants were accustomed to perform the rice harvest operation in two stages: first they cut the top of the stalks, about a dozen centimetres below the ear, and later cut the straw down to soil level. The reason for this labour-expensive method is the desire to gather and garner the ears with the least possible delay, since this is the part of the harvest that is most precious.

In the same delta a family of four persons, two working adults and two children old enough to help, was insufficient to maintain more than 700 square metres (about one-sixth of an acre) of tobacco. The labour requirement was of an extraordinary intensity; the application of liquid human manure, plant by plant, was very time-consuming; and in order not to damage the leaves, the removal of aphids was effected by children armed with sticks, on the end of which was a ball of sticky glue.

The relentless energy of the peasants was most movingly apparent when disaster overtook the crops; there was an immediate effort to replant, that was frustrated only by the lack of seedlings.

IRRIGATION

In general, most wet ricefields made do with just rain water, that remained stagnant in the fields. This arrangement was inconvenient, for the paddy harvest was greater if the field dried out occasionally, but it had the great merit that the muddy and stagnant water was hostile to the development of the larvae of malaria-carrying mosquitoes. Nevertheless, it was rare for a rice harvest to be successfully achieved without the peasants, with much toil and sweat, having to carry water to the fields.

In order to bring water to the ricefields, from an adjacent canal or pond, the peasants developed several simple devices, light and easy to assemble from bamboo and basketwork (also made from bamboo). The most widespread type was the ladle, in its most rudimentary form simply a hand-operated scoop. More economical of human effort was a single ladle suspended from a tripod. A ladle on the end of a rope, operated by two people, enabled a greater lift to be attained. For larger volumes of water, more elaborate machines, such as pedal-norias (Figs. 6.1 and 6.2) were used. Using the tripod-ladle, a peasant working for seven hours a day, at the (unusually rapid) rate of twenty-two scoops a minute, could raise 100 square metres of water 40 centimetres; or, to give another example, the covering of one hectare to a depth of 10 centimetres, by this method, would take at least twelve days. This, however, is in theory only, for in practice the single tripod-ladle would not be used to irrigate so large an area.

It was often necessary to lift water more than 40 centimetres. In this case the peasants would employ a succession of two-man ladles, lifting the water step by step. Often the water had to pass through several ricefields, and this gave rise to many arguments, and since the water was much in demand in times of drought, to many fraudulent abstractions. It was a custom in Tonkinese villages for eight inhabitants of the third 'table' to be designated to watch over the irrigation of the ricefields. If, through negligence, they allowed so much water to flow away that it was no longer possible to plant out even the lowest fields, the whole 'third table' group was punished by a fine of five 'ligatures' per person.[1]

Conflicts over water use were frequent. The owner of a low-level paddyfield could irrigate it for nothing by making a breach in the dyke of the field above, and without much risk, for rats or crabs could always be blamed for the creation of the breach. But such occurrences would give rise to complaints, disputes, reprisals and prolonged conflicts between families.

MANURE

Far Eastern lands are not all naturally endowed with great fertility; soils or hill-slopes, in China and Vietnam, are acid and lacking in plant food; the carefully cultivated terraces that border the Japanese plains have unproductive soils. It must not be thought that all Japanese soils developed on volcanic ash are rich, for much of the volcanic debris is acid and makes a very poor soil parent. Moreover, the land has been cultivated for a very long time, and not merely once a year but often two or even three times; surely it must have been drained of its fertility by over-use? But this is not all: the peasants leave neither straw nor vegetable debris on the surface, and they even pull up the roots of cereals; everything is used as fuel, and the soil is thus deprived of organic matter.

Chinese soil, however, is better manured than that of India, for example, for the Chinese peasant is acutely aware of the necessity for manure, and he does not burn dung as fuel. Moreover, the Chinese have no qualms about using human excreta, unlike the Indians who regard them as impure. Chinese agriculture has succeeded in developing a manuring technique that assures the best crop yields.

Human manure is of two kinds, liquid and solid. In the court-yard of every house is a large jar for the collection of urine; the

---

[1] At municipal feasts, the inhabitants were arranged in a hierarchy of 'tables'. Coins (the Chinese 'cash'), pierced with a hole, were tied together with a string, a certain number of 'cashes' formed a 'ligature'.

Fig. 6.2   A pedal-noria (from a seventeenth-century Chinese document).
Water is raised from a river into a canal that feeds a newly planted ricefield

smell of ammonia arising therefrom is the first impression that greets a visitor to a Red River delta village. Solid excreta are carefully piled up, and when mixed with water make a precious manure that is spread sparingly around delicate plants. Someone has calculated that in the whole of the Far East, fifty years ago, 182 million tonnes of human manure each year put back into the soil 150 000 tonnes of phosphorus, 360 000 of potassium and 1 200 000 tonnes of nitrogen. The transport of this material is responsible for the unpleasant odours that pervade the roads and fields. Around the villages, human manure is an item of trade. Urban night-soil is carried out every morning, and at the crack of dawn a convoy of muck-carriers streams out towards the surrounding countryside, within a distance of perhaps 30 km from the town. Documents dating from the ninth century AD refer to 'emptiers of urine jars' and 'scavengers of cesspools'. Some villages made a speciality of this traffic. Near to Hanoi was a village of scavengers, who collected night-soil, mixed it with earth in large pits and then sold the mixture to peasants who came from villages as far away as 10 or 15 km. These peasants then walked back home, carrying two large panniers of manure suspended from a yoke across their shoulders. This village was rightly proud of its trade; a young girl who took as a husband a man not practising as a muck-vendor would have been regarded as having married beneath her station.

Farm manure is of several kinds. Cattle are few in number, and as there is no available straw for litter, little manure is produced of the kind that is so carefully conserved elsewhere. Children search the footpaths for dung, which they scoop up with the shoulderblade of a buffalo; and when buffaloes are used to turn norias or mills, a child will walk behind them, catching the droppings in a basket before they reach the ground. Pig manure is considered by the Tonkin peasants to be especially rich, and so that it may not be scattered indiscriminately by the animals they are kept in pigsties, fed with rice bran and banana stalks.

All kinds of residues are carefully used: in Chinese mulberry plantations, peasants will bury at the foot of each tree the silkworm droppings, chrysalis cases, and half-eaten leaves; everything that has been taken from the soil and from the tree by the use of its leaves is returned, except the silk.

Much use is made of the mud from ponds, rivers and canals. Sometimes a layer of mud several centimetres deep may be spread over a ricefield that is regarded as exhausted. The bed of a canal is dredged with a longhandled scoop, the material being dumped into a floating sampan that transports it to its destination, where perhaps 200 or 300 tonnes of mud per hectare may be spread over the field — and the whole operation is done by hand. An even better example could be seen in Chekiang province, where the peasants sometimes strip off the topsoil from a ricefield, dump it in the canal, and then dredge the canal bed to recover the enriched material. In the drier parts of China peasants take topsoil from their fields to the village, spread it out over the farmyard, where it will be enriched by organic matter and aerated by the treading of people and animals, and then replace it in the field. In this case the transporting will be done by packanimals. The Chinese peasant is well aware that the mudbricks that are used in building the k'ang, the oven and the stove in their houses in the north are rich in fertilising elements because of the soot that impregnates them; when therefore a k'ang that is no longer in use is demolished, they crush the old bricks and spread them over the fields.

The use of green manure is also well understood by Far Eastern peasants; they bury leaves that they have gathered in the forest or on the hillsides. Japanese peasants would take green manure to their ricefields when the rice was already well advanced; walking with their legs on either side of a row of riceplants, they would proceed with bent backs, burying leaves and herbage and stamping the earth underneath their feet. The Chinese knew that leguminous plants enriched the soil with nitrogen, and they had the bright idea of cultivating a clover (*Astragalus sinensis*). Sometimes this would be ploughed in, but alternatively it might be cut, then spread over the bed of a river or canal and saturated with mud. After twenty or thirty days of fermentation, the resulting compost would be spread over the fields. More refined processes could produce composts of very great richness; in Kiangsu the peasants dig pits where they mix clover, canal mud and night-soil purchased from Shanghai. At the expense of vast amounts of human labour such techniques enabled the fields to be manured without using too much land for growing clover, and the resulting soils would yield two or three crops a year.

The Tonkin peasants used green manure on wet ricefields, particularly those that gave two harvests a year. *Azolla* is an aquatic fern that floats on the surface of the flooded field and dies in April when the temperature rises. It performs three functions: it slows down evaporation by shading the water surface, it disappears at the time when it could hinder the growth of the rice (which ripens in June) and it makes a useful green manure. Curiously enough, most of the peasants did not know how to keep it alive during the hot season, and when, in November, the time arrived to spread the *azolla* over the ricefields, they had to buy plants from a village which possessed (and jealously guarded) the secret of the survival and reproduction of the *azolla* in the dry season. The people of this village sold their first plants at a high price to other villages, where they were multiplied and sold again. The one village that held the closely guarded secret was in a monopolistic position, and its economic relations with its neighbours were slight but delicate. A characteristic, indeed, of the economic life of the Far Eastern countryside, was the small total volume of business, in comparison with the number and complexity of the individual transactions.

The quantity of manure applied to the land by various means is considerable, probably not far short of a dozen tonnes to the hectare; even so, it is certain that the soil of China has insufficient, for it has to yield harvests that are too unvaried, being almost entirely cereals, and too closely spaced.

MULTIPLE CROPPING

Everything leads the Far Eastern peasant to get more than one harvest into the twelve months: population density, the smallness of the holdings, the fear of famine, the ingenuity of the techniques and the passion for hard work. The climate, it is true, has not been unhelpful, and the more southerly regions could easily get two or even three harvests in a year, as in the Yangtse area and even more so in southern China. But in northern China only one harvest was possible, though even here, in some favoured spots, the main cotton harvest could be followed by a catch-crop including such varied items as soya, beans, sesamum, potatoes, sweet potatoes, millet, tobacco, buckwheat, hemp, maize, cabbage or onions. In general, in China, about half the fields yielded two crops a year; in Japan, only one-third of the culti-vated area produced two harvests, but this figure rose to 95 per cent in the southernmost parts of the country, and similarly in southern Korea. But it is not easy to calculate the percentage of the land producing more than one harvest in twelve months. The case of the fields that produce one rice crop and one wheat crop a year is simple, but what about the fields in which one sees several crops growing at once, being harvested at overlapping periods? In the same field there may be cotton, maize and beans. Often the Chinese peasant will sow cotton seeds among the ripen-ing wheat, and will sow a second lot after the wheat has been harvested. Similar methods, more akin to horticulture, may actually produce from selected fields not two crops a year but four or five. But five crops in twelve months will not represent five times the value of one good harvest.

The practice of manuring reduced the necessity for crop rota-tions. In northern China wheat was sown continuously until the yield became too low; then they turned to maize and sorghum, plentifully manured. In the Yangtse area the general rule was a winter crop of wheat or barley, with beans or peas, and summer rice; only where the soil was unsuitable for paddy were summer crops raised of soya, sweet potatoes, maize or cotton. South of the Yangtse basin, double-cropping of rice predominated. With a little imagination one could perhaps discern an element of ration-ality in some of these crop successions: for example, a shallow-rooted crop followed by one with deep roots; then a cleaning (hoed) crop, followed by a leguminous crop. But the truth is that the whole business was much less systematic. The Far Eastern peasant must make certain of his food supply from year to year, if not indeed from month to month. How could he be sure that a fallow designed to enrich the soil would actually result in a better harvest the next year? In any case he would not be there to know, because he would have died from starvation meanwhile. As we have seen, it was the practice of careful manuring that avoided the necessity for either rotations or fallows.

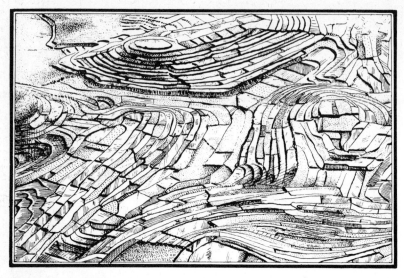

Fig. 6.3   Paddyfields in Kwantung. In this favoured area, the entire surface has been transformed into wet ricefields, not only the valley bottom, but the slopes as well

TECHNIQUES OF RICE-GROWING

Rice-growing, the most important peasant activity in the Far East, has provided a multitude of opportunities for the exercise of ingenuity and acute observation. The varieties grown are innumerable, and there are many in every locality. They are not grown indiscriminately, for each one has qualities that respond to particular environmental conditions: greater or less resistance to drought, ability to grow in deep water ('floating rice'), liability to lodging, quick or slow ripening, degree of tolerance towards brackish water, and so on. The peasant is well aware that a quick-ripening strain is less productive than one that has a more normal growth period; nevertheless he does not hesitate to plant such varieties if he feels that the harvest is likely to be harmed by flooding or drought. He plants rice that will mature at staggered dates, so as to ensure a succession of harvests. Along the paths followed by the sheaf-carrying harvesters, he will plant a belt several feet wide of a variety that will mature before the main harvest; in this way he will avoid losses through the treading

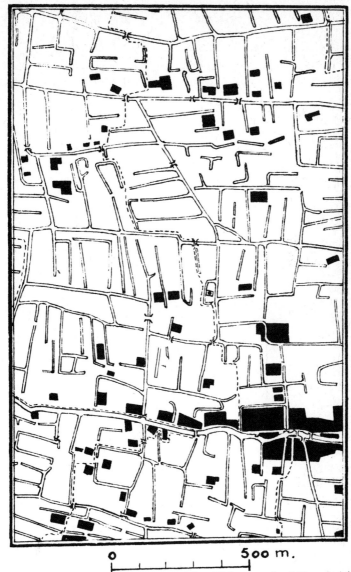

0   500 m.

Fig. 6.4   A landscape in the Yangtse delta, 50 km south of Shanghai (from a map of the Wangpoo Conservancy Board used by G. B. Cressey in 'The Fenghsien landscape, a fragment of the Yangtse Delta', *Geogr. Review*, 1936, 396—413). Houses in black: a dispersed settlement with a commercial nucleus. Innumerable canals (double lines), and a few paths (pecked lines)

down of the plants and the stealing of handfuls of ripe ears (Figs. 6.3 and 6.4).

The planting out of rice is a good example of a refined agricultural technique. It is understandable that on the edge of a pond or the receding flood of a river, the peasant will find it advantageous to pull up his rice plants and replant them on the edge of the water. This is a simple matter: without replanting he will get no harvest. But the regular ricefields can be managed simply by sowing, without replanting; which is not an indispensable process. Replanting is thus clearly a deliberate effort at more intensive production. Moreover, it results in a great economy in seed, perhaps 50 or 100 kg per hectare compared with direct sowing. Since the total area of riceland harvested at various times of the year in the Far East is of the order of 30 million hectares, this means an economy of between 1.5 and 3 million tonnes of rice.

Replanting enables the riceplants, during their first few weeks, to grow in a well-manured soil and under constant care. Once replanted they are not liable to be choked by weeds, for they will be well in advance of the weeds that arise from seeds. Replanting is also a necessary element in multiple cropping, for it reduces the time during which a field is occupied by a rice crop. Lastly, it would often be impossible, at sowing time, to sow fields that were too dry or still flooded, and replanting enables the ricefields to be brought into just the right hydraulic condition to receive the plants.

The preparation of the seedbed is carried out with the utmost care and great skill, so as to ensure the best growth of the plants. As a result, the fields of young rice present a carpet of uniform, shiny green, as lustrous and velvety as a beautiful English lawn.

But what a labour it all represents! It is usually done in midsummer heat; the sun glints on the surface of the water and hurts the eyes of the planters. For ten hours a day, with backs bent, they make holes for the plants in the mud, taking care to move in a straight line. In Japan, a string with beads at regular intervals, moved each time a row is completed, enables the planters to keep a perfect alignment. This terribly hard work, the worst task of the whole year, was done by women in Japan and in Tonkin, but by men in China.

CHAPTER 7

THE COUNTRYSIDE THROUGH THE YEAR

He who kills a cow will become a cow in the next life.

Chinese saying

If it does not rain on the eighth day of the fourth month, I shall have to abandon plough and harrow, bury the rice plants, and wait until the tenth month, in order to get a good harvest and relieve my hunger.

Vietnamese popular song

Both time and space were dominated in the Far East by the sheer relentlessness of human labour. Throughout the entire year the rural population toiled in the fields with but little relaxation, tilling, ploughing, manuring, sowing, weeding, irrigating, planting, harvesting. Even the intervals between agricultural tasks were occupied in fishing, fuel-collecting, repairs to houses, preparation of foodstuffs, or in industry or trade. The landscape bore but few traces of the last two activities; its entire appearance, in the inhabited and cultivated areas, reflected its complete occupation by the peasantry; its every facet, moulded by the activities of the cultivator, expressed his efforts in the minutest detail.

THE AGRICULTURAL CALENDAR

Naturally enough, climatic variation caused differences in the rhythm of agriculture. But throughout, there is one general

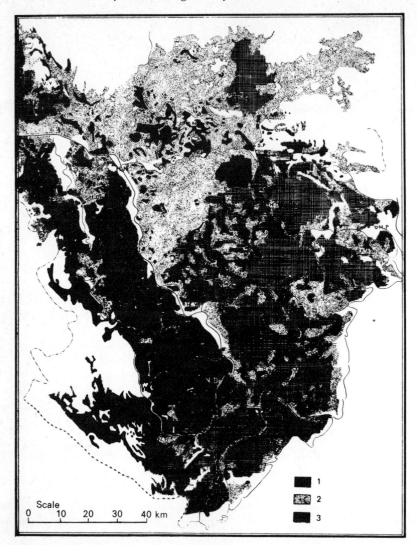

Fig. 7.1   **Rice cultivation in the Red River delta.**
Key: 1. ricefields with only one (the fifth month) harvest; 2. ricefields with only one (tenth month) harvest; 3. ricefields yielding two harvests

characteristic, the diversity and multiplicity of the agricultural tasks.

In the Red River delta the agricultural year ends at the beginning of *December*, with the main rice harvest. But the rice is hardly garnered before the next farming cycle begins, and the peasants prepare for their next crops. In the lowest lands, where the depth of floodwater has prevented rainy season cropping, the 'fifth month' rice must be urgently planted out (Fig. 7.1); it will be ripe by May, before the monsoon rains bring further floods. Also in December, the peasants must prepare the ground for the dry season crops, either in the dried-out paddyfields or in areas that are only used for dry cultivation, particularly the beds of temporarily dried-up rivers. The land is ploughed, the clods are broken up with a mallet, and ridges are built up for planting taro, castor oil, sweet potatoes and beans; and all the plants are carefully and separately manured.

The main work in *January* is the planting out of the 'fifth month' rice on the two-harvest paddyfields, which are slightly higher in elevation than the one-harvest fields, where planting takes place in December. The planting of dry-season crops continues, with the sowing of maize in association with beans, soya and sweet potatoes. Already some crops are ready for harvesting, such as arrowroot and potatoes that were planted in September on the higher lands where the rice had been harvested at the end of August. Sweet potatoes are quickly replanted on the same land, after breaking down the ridges and reconstructing them on the site of the intervening furrows. And the vegetable harvest continues.

February is the first month in the Chinese calendar; there is a brief respite, almost the only time of the year that the peasant relaxes without looking for work. Over the whole of the Far East, the peasantry celebrates according to its means, or even beyond its means, for frequently the money has to be borrowed to pay for the expenses of the New Year revels. It is a good augury for the new year to start with relative plenty. The peasant eats, drinks, pays visits and receives guests, plays with his children, dresses up in his best clothes, and lets off crackers and draws bows and arrows on the floor of his courtyard to frighten off evil spirits. But with all this, the fields are not entirely neglected; the dry crops are given a second dressing of manure, tobacco is planted out, and vegetables are harvested.

In *March*, the main preoccupation is with the fifth month rice

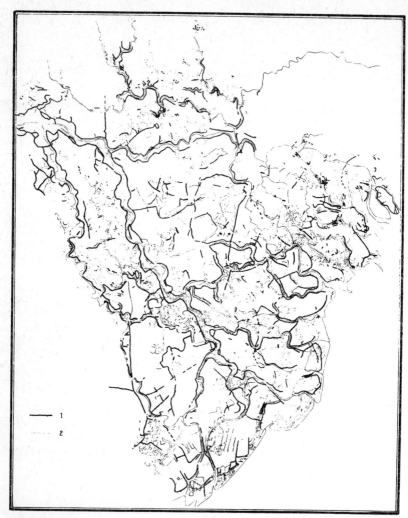

Fig. 7.2   Hydrological control of a delta by man: the Red River delta (scale 1/1M).
Key: 1. principal dykes; 2. secondary dykes

crop, and this remains in the foreground until June. Weeds are hoed out or pulled up by hand; the floodwater is stirred manually; manure is applied; the dykes are inspected and made watertight, and any water that has been lost is with difficulty made

Fig. 7.3   **Harrowing a ricefield (from an eighteenth-century Chinese drawing). A buffalo pulls the harrow, which reduces the soil to an impalpable mud. The peasant is wearing a waterproof garment made of straw**

good. On the higher lands, arrowroot and manioc are planted out, beans and castor-oil seeds are harvested, and sweet potatoes planted on the ground thus vacated.

April is not very different. There may be a second weeding of the ricefields, and since this is the flowering season for rice, when the crop needs the maximum amount of water, it may be necessary for irrigation to be applied. At this time the fifth month ricefields give off an odour like that emitted by a pot of boiling rice; to the peasants it is a very agreeable smell. During the month sweet potatoes planted in January are lifted, and sesamum is sown.

There is more hard work in *May*. The tenth month ricefields, that carry only one crop a year, are ploughed and harrowed (Fig. 7.3), and the seedbeds are prepared. On some of these that have been prepared earlier, on the higher lands that are subject to drought, an early crop will be sown that will be replanted later

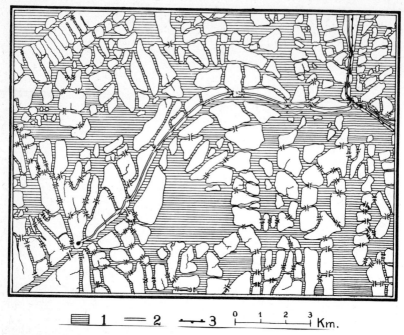

Fig. 7.4   An amphibious landscape in the Yangtse delta, south of Lake Tai (from Hsiano Tung Fui, *Peasant Life in China*, London, 1939, 14). **The rice-fields have been reclaimed from the lakes. This is a much more aquatic landscape than that of Fig. 6.3**
Key: 1. lakes and rivers; 2. roads; 3. railway

on so as to ripen in August. 'Three moons' rice is planted out now, to ripen in July. The harvest of beans and castor-oil seeds continues, and millet is also gathered in.

In Tonkin, as in China, the month of *June* is a period of strenuous labour. In Tonkin the fifth month rice harvest has begun at the end of May, in a frantic effort to garner the grain before the heavy rains bring floods; a single day's delay may mean the loss of a large part of the crop. Rural wage rates are at their maximum at this time. If the rice has ripened without the water having been drained off, the harvest has to take place under very disagreeable and wet conditions. Often the sheaves must be piled up on punts made of woven bamboo, rendered as impermeable as possible, but it is difficult to find a place to put

**Fig. 7.5   Threshing paddy (from an eighteenth-century Chinese drawing).
The sheaves are bashed against a large stone placed on a straw mat**

them in this aquatic landscape. The harvesters are soaked to the
skin, and their legs are eaten by leeches.

There are many other harvests in June: taro and sweet potato

Fig. 7.6   A hydraulic pounder (from a fourteenth-century Chinese document). Water falls into a large ladle; when this is full, it raises the hammer; when it empties, the hammer falls on to the grain that is to be husked

that were planted in March, also cotton and maize. Tobacco leaves are picked. Sesamum is uprooted, and with the rice hardly out of the ground, more sesamum is sown for harvest in late July, before the preparation for the tenth month rice crop begins. The land is prepared for fresh crops; after the rice is harvested, the two-crop ricefields are tilled and the seedbeds sown.

July is almost as busy a month as June. Many fields must be ploughed and harrowed, immediately after the fifth month rice harvest, for planting out tenth month rice; this is the time for planting out the most important crop of the whole year. Irrigation water must be applied if the rains do not yield enough, and this may add appreciably to the strenuous labour of rice-planting. The last of the dry-season crops are gathered in; sweet potatoes, jute, taro, indigo. In the coastal regions the cutting of reeds begins, to provide the essential raw material for basketwork.

In *August* the replanting of the tenth month rice is completed, and the three moons rice crop is harvested; but in general this is a relatively slack period after the hard work of May, June and July.

The pace quickens again in *September*. The tenth month rice is in flower, and must be irrigated if the rains are insufficient. The paddy must be weeded, the water stirred and manure applied; and any early ripening varieties must be reaped.

In *October* the main rice harvest begins on the one-crop paddies, on the higher lands that are already threatened with drying out. Sugarcane, grown on the banks of rivers, is cut, and raw brown sugar is prepared. Sweet potatoes are planted on ricefields that have already been harvested. The seedbeds for the next fifth month rice crop are prepared.

November sees the tenth month rice harvest in full swing; a cheerful month, for it is the best time of the whole year. The great heat has moderated, the rains have ceased, the air is dry and clear, and the light is almost Mediterranean. The harvest work is quite pleasant on the dried-out fields; with no danger from storms and floods, it can be carried on at a more leisurely pace. The sheaves are thrashed by one of the usual Far Eastern methods; treading out under foot, or under a roller, beating with a flail, or shelling the ears by hand in the case of special varieties or grain to be used for seed. Sometimes, perhaps, a sheaf loosely tied with cord to two bamboo handles will be battered against a

Fig. 7.7 A hand-operated mill for husking rice (from an eighteenth-century Chinese drawing)

Fig. 7.8   A balancing-pole pounder for polishing rice (from an eighteenth-century Chinese drawing)

stone. From the end of November, the low-lying paddyfields, still under water, will be ploughed in preparation for their only crop, fifth month rice; and the seedbeds for this will be sown. Manioc will be harvested, and in its place sugarcane will be planted, for harvesting in the following October.

This detailed account of the agricultural year in the Red River delta shows clearly that there is no simple subdivision into a summer (wet) monsoon and a winter (dry) monsoon season. The succession of agricultural operations has many subsidiary rhythms. True, Tonkin is favoured by temperatures that sustain all-the-year-round vegetative activity, and by slight winter rains that prevent an interruption of agricultural work (even though irrigation may still be necessary to produce better crops). In northwest China the winter is too cold for agriculture, and is a time of rural unemployment, for the peasants have no cattle that might, if reserves of forage had been accumulated during the summer, keep them occupied.

THE RURAL LANDSCAPE

The fragmentation, the minute land holdings, the absence of pastoralism and the dominance of wet rice cultivation all result in a rural landscape very different from those of western Europe. The latter are also peasant landscapes, but of a quite different nature. In the Far East one seeks in vain the Normandy grass-lands, the hedges and trees of the *bocage*, the vineyards, and the open fields with the strip-cultivation that recalls the medieval three-field system. The European, surprised by a new world, will experience many disappointments if he expects to find the land-scapes of his childhood. If in his homeland he enjoyed walking across fields, lying in the long grass, gathering ripe berries from a hedge or the occasional grape from a vineyard, he will find no such pleasures available in the Far East. Nothing edible is avail-able for the picking; all the berries and fruits have been assidu-ously gathered by eager hands, even before they were ripe; and in any case fruit trees are something of a rarity.

It is impossible to wander across the fields, for they are paddy-fields in which the trespasser would sink up to his knees. And as for lying in the grass — impossible because there is no grass. No forest, no woods; the cemeteries are the only parts of the flat countryside that are not given over to cultivation. No chance here of encountering a great lumbering farm cart, a herd of cattle drinking at the pond, the majestic movements of the sower, or the graceful sweep of the reaper. In the Far East there are neither carts nor herds; and there is no grace about the movement of the sower, who with bent back, digs little holes in the ground and drops the seeds in. The scythe is not part of the peasant's equipment; the only comparable rhythmic movement is the slow motion of the peasant who goes through the ricefield swinging a large open basket on the end of a long handle, collecting edible and harmful insects from the plants.

Many visitors wishing to penetrate the recesses of the Far Eastern countryside have been discouraged by the rough and narrow paths that follow the sinuous field boundaries and are much longer than is necessary; and they could well have been exhausted from the lack of convenient halts; inns were few and far between, and very poor. After a long walk one would only find an uncomfortable shelter in a dilapidated temple; the food would be monotonous and unappetising, and the washing water muddy. Other mishaps might befall the traveller and colour his impressions; he might slide into a wet ricefield, or get bogged down in a manure pit concealed by too thin an earth cover, or be thrown off a capsizing ferry.

To appreciate the beauty of the Far Eastern rural landscape, one must forget the West completely and accept the different standards of this corner of Asia. The ricefields have a varied charm that easily surpasses in its delicacy the monotonous fields of potatoes or wheat that one finds in Europe. After the replanting, when the plants are still small, the paddyfield plain is a chequerboard of mirrors, the water reflecting the varied shadow of the clouds and the changing angle of the sun. Seen from a neighbouring hill this watery landscape, with its varied and changing illumination, has a captivating charm of its own. It is not like the vast expanse of the sea, nor the grandeur which, to our Western eyes, comes from satisfying proportions or a harmonious grouping of lines and shapes. The charm is in the immense variety of subtle nuances, the mottlings that accompany slight variations in the wind as it rustles the frail blades of the riceplants, and the infinite play of light and colour.

When the rice has grown so that it covers the plain entirely, a new landscape appears, more stable and without the constant changes produced by sunlight, clouds and wind; it is an immense green carpet, that hides the water underneath and gives an impression of strength and prosperity. The only hark-back to the previous landscape is the patches of different greens produced by the different types of rice planted and the precise stage of development reached by each, that depends partly on the amount of irrigation water provided. With the approach of the harvest, the ricefields take on the hue of a Western wheatfield. The finest golden colours are seen with the approach of a thunderstorm: the enormous black mass of a cumulonimbus cloud, topped with a white anvil and fringed by sparkling cumulus, overshadows a plain illuminated by a last ray of sunshine.

When the land surface becomes hilly but still exploitable, the rice terraces present the viewer with a series of sinuous steps that look like cyclopean constructions superimposed on the natural relief forms; concave and convex slopes are lost in the regular staircase of terraces.

On the approach to a village, a more minutely fragmented landscape appears: a pond with turbid water covered in duckweed, a buffalo-wallow, clusters of bamboos, a few trees, and a horn-spired temple. These elements may be grouped in a most harmonious fashion, with a delicate blending of colours; but the earth itself is trodden by people and littered with debris, and the pond is muddy (though it may also be teeming with fish).

There is nothing, in the plains of the Far East, to recall the clear, green streams of western Europe, with their tree-clad banks. The rivers are laden with debris, that gives them names like Yellow River, Red River, or, by an astonishing misuse of words, Blue River. Enclosed by dykes, and swollen by the incoming tide, these great rivers, in their lower courses, wind majestically through the landscape, to which they contribute a kind of fourth dimension, measuring the march of time by their unceasing flow. Sometimes their opaque and gently ruffled surface reflects most beautifully the rays of the setting sun — the 'roses of the Red River'; but they never look pure and limpid like the smaller, unpolluted rivers of Europe.

Except for a comparatively few plains, the landscapes of Japan are different. The ever-present mountains, the development of the coastline, the striking forms of the volcanoes, and the abundance and beauty of the trees make up a countryside that is more immediately attractive than that of China. The Japanese love of nature leads them to respect landscapes and trees; large parts of the country look as if they had been laid out by a landscape architect, while the characteristic cleanliness and tidiness make the rural scene even more attractive. Aside from the great classical landscapes which are places of national pilgrimage, the ordinary countryside offers a thousand delightful aspects, and in almost every village a temple raises its upturned roofs above the thatched houses, which are gay in the spring with blooming irises and the foliage of the cedars (*Cryptomeria*). The orange groves and their ripe fruit add charm to the surroundings of the Inland Sea in winter; clover, which is used as green manure, covers the ricefields in southern Japan in spring with a velvety reddish carpet, which contrasts with the pale yellow of the fields of mustard; in autumn the 'kaki' orchards (persimmon – *Diospyros*) are laden with red fruit. The tea terraces of Kyoto and Shizuoka, with their large bushes trimmed like box trees, are perhaps at their best under a snow cover. Unfortunately some of these charming features are becoming obsolete. Already the coastlines between Tokyo and Nagoya, and around the Inland Sea, have lost their character; they have been invaded by more aggressive forms of occupation, and by organised leisure.

CHAPTER 8

CROPS, LIVESTOCK AND FISH

The mandarins pray for rain, and rain falls. What does
that signify? For me, there is no relation between the
two facts. The rain would have fallen just the same,
without the prayers.

Hsun Ching (3rd century BC)

AGRICULTURAL PRODUCTION

There is an overwhelming preference for the cultivation of
cereals, which form the basis of Far Eastern food supply.
Tuberous plants are far behind. This was natural enough when
the coolest parts of the Far East had no tuber crop worthy of
interest, though it is rather less so since the availability of the
potato. The yield per hectare of potatoes exceeds that of wheat
or millet, but nevertheless the peasants prefer their traditional
cereal diet. The growing of vegetables, fruit and industrial plants
is of minor importance; forage crops are negligible and meadows
non-existent.

Rice-growing is the principal occupation. Wet rice probably
covers 30 million hectares (including the double-cropped areas)
and the harvest amounts to some 70 million tonnes. Except in
northern China (Manchuria) rice absorbs the greater part of the
peasant's agricultural effort and controls the rhythm of the farming calendar; other forms of cropping have to give way to the
demands of rice culture. Thus the Tonkin peasants grow cotton
in the dry season and harvest it at the beginning of the monsoon
rains; this is most unfortunate, for both flowering and picking
take place at the least favourable time of the year, when flowers
and bolls alike suffer from the rainstorms. But what else can they

do, when the fields must be available from July to November for the wet season rice crop?

There are many reasons for the dominance of rice among the cereal crops. Because of its growth in standing water its yield is much higher than any non-irrigated cereal that could be grown on the same plot. During the decade 1930—40, the average Chinese wheat harvest was estimated at 1000 kg per hectare, that of rice at 3000 kg. Rice certainly requires more labour than wheat, but the peasants have a vast capacity for work and often appear underemployed. Wet rice thus has a most valuable ability to give high yields; it will make do with quite poor soils provided that there is ample irrigation water. Thanks to the replanting operation, it requires relatively little seed and it occupies the land for but a short time. Because it is grown in water it is less subject to drought or excessive rain than the other cereals (Fig. 8.1).

The 'secondary' cereals in the Far Eastern countries produced, all told, about as great a tonnage as that of rice, some 70 million tonnes. But these 140 million tonnes of harvested grain scarcely sufficed for the needs of a population which, even in 1940, numbered over 500 million. What then is the present situation, with a population approaching 1000 million? Has cereal production expanded at a similar rate? To a certain extent, yes, but production falls short of demand. China must annually import several million tonnes of wheat. And it would appear that quantities of Russian cereals have been purchased for use in the Red River delta of North Vietnam. The most important food plant after cereals, though very far behind, was the sweet potato (*Ipomea batatas*), which yielded about 30 million tonnes of tubers annually. For many Chinese and Japanese peasants this was a staple item in the diet; the tubers were sliced and dried, and thus could be consumed throughout the year. The peasants did not like them very much, for they are somewhat indigestible, but they recognised the advantage of a food that eases the pangs of hunger for a long time.

Apart from cereals and sweet potatoes, the other food crops play but a very minor role. The consumption of sugar in the Far East was very low, and it played but a negligible part in the calorie intake; and this despite the cultivation of cane and the knowledge of sugar-refining. In the circumstances within which

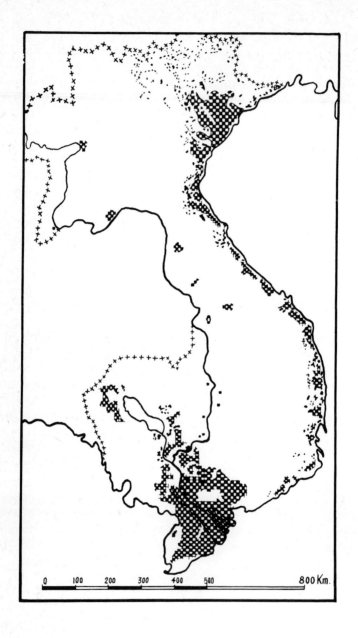

the peasants are confined by their own civilisation, this is most unfortunate, for no other crop can rival sugarcane in calorific value, and a yield of 10 000 kg of sugar per hectare could be obtained in twelve months. It is true that only Vietnam, south-eastern China and Kyushu are climatically suitable for sugarcane, but even in these areas it does not have the importance it merits. The new civilisation that is remodelling life in these parts should certainly look into this question, not merely with a view to giving the sugarcane a larger share in the cropping system but also, in the appropriate areas, to developing the cultivation of sugar beet.

Peas and beans contribute protein and fat to a Far Eastern diet that is noticeably deficient in these elements. The most wide-spread of these pulses is the soya bean, which is eaten in a thousand different ways: it may be just boiled, but when ground to flour it can be used for making cheeses, widely consumed, that could be mistaken for the white cheeses of western Europe. Fermented soya cheese, called stinking cheese in Suchow province, is not unlike a ripe Roquefort in smell and taste. Sprouted soya is a green vegetable, rich in vitamins, that can be obtained all the year round (the 'bean shoots' on the menus of our Chinese restaurants). This happy 'discovery' long preceded the use of Brussels chicory (endive) in the West, for the same purpose; but there is much more nourishment in the young shoots of the soya plant.

Soya is used for the preparation of a sauce that relieves the insipid taste of rice and at the same time is rich in protein. Soya, indeed, has an advantage over other beans in containing high quality protein and fats, including lecithin. Soya cake, the residue from the extraction of a cooking oil, makes an excellent organic manure; but it would be more sensible to feed it to animals, whose dung could then be applied to the soil. The soya bean is one of the triumphs of Chinese agriculture; the discovery

---

Fig. 8.1 Ricefields in Vietnam, Laos and Cambodia. This map clearly demonstrates the close confinement of intensive agriculture and high population densities. It brings out the surprising economic structure of Vietnam: the Tonkin and Cochinchina areas linked by a narrow fringe of ricefields, the importance of the fringe being exaggerated on a map of this scale

and perfection of its qualities and uses are the result of perseverance and skill. Soya cultivation has been adopted into the agricultural systems of the United States, where it yields oil and cake and enters into the preparation of many alimentary products such as chocolate, biscuits and animals feedstuffs. It is somewhat ironical that China, so little interested in livestock farming, should have given to the pastoral industries of the United States so precious a food for animals.

The other oil-yielding plants give but small quantities of cooking oils, but some of them, like mustard, sesamum, ground-nuts and cotton, are the most important sources of fats that China possesses.

The production of green vegetables is at a modest level. These vegetarian peoples of the Far East actually consume few fresh vegetables. The most widespread vegetable in China, the Chinese cabbage, is actually a form of mustard plant. The Japanese grow a great variety of edible roots, the most remarkable of which is the *daikon*, a huge radish which is cut into slices and pickled; and they use plums pickled in vinegar to season rice dishes. The Tonkin peasants use a curious vegetable, the hydropire; this is the stem of an aquatic plant, in the interior of which there are parasitic fungi that give it an exquisite flavour.

Fruit growing in China plays but a small part in the general agricultural system and in the normal diet; but it has not been neglected by the Chinese horticulturalists. We may perhaps regard as rather unnecessary their search for strange forms of citron (like those called 'Hand of Buddha'); but they have certainly succeeded in obtaining useful hybrids of the citrus family, like those grown in Fukien which have the taste of a mandarine and the juiciness of an orange. In a reorganised China it will be necessary to improve both the production of fruit (by using neglected hillsides) and its consumption (by providing easier and less costly transport and raising the general standard of life).

TEA

Tea is a plant as characteristic of the Far East as rice, bamboo and mulberry. Tea growing, which represents China's greatest success in the field of arboriculture, is well adapted to the particular conditions that Far Eastern civilisation has imposed upon mankind. On the one hand, it makes no demands on the soil; give it something light and friable to grow in and it will not require great fertility. As a result it can use neglected hillsides that are of no use for growing food crops. On the other hand, and particularly during the picking season, it makes very heavy demands on human labour, that Far Eastern villages are well equipped to provide. It is an advantage, too, from the labour point of view, that the harvest is not effected at one fell swoop but is relatively prolonged.

It was the Chinese who perfected the art of preparing the leaves and making the infusion that we know as tea. It depends on the maturity of the leaves, on the extent to which they are withered, and on the degree of heat-drying; the result can be either green tea or black tea. As with sericulture, it all derives from a treasure-house of patient observation combined with technical skill. The making of different qualities of Chinese tea is a highly specialised occupation; tea-tasters are every bit as skilled as the wine-tasters of the Western world. Whole books have been written on the infusion of tea and the way to boil the water. The finest tea, according to the Chinese, is devoid of acridity; it should leave a taste in the mouth for several minutes after being drunk. It has nothing in common with the thick brown brew of a London teashop. Chinese tea is drunk without milk or sugar. There is a great art in associating varieties of tea with sources of water which suit them best. Chen Fu, an eighteenth-century Chinese writer, describes a refined and delicate method of making tea: place a small muslin bag containing tea into the flower of a lotus, in the evening when the flower is about to close up; next morning, when the flower opens again take it out; infused in rainwater, the tea will have a subtle aroma. It has been justly remarked that the most deeply rooted peasantries of the Old World, the Mediterranean and the Chinese, have developed, through careful selection of plants and skilful techniques, two drinks, wine and tea, which are the hallmarks of an advanced civilisation. This comparison will not satisfy the drinkers of cheap red wine, but it is valid enough.

Fig. 8.2 A female silk-spinner (from an eighteenth-century Chinese drawing)

SILK

Like the production of tea, sericulture is very well adapted to the conditions of life in the Far East; and it happens also that the climate is favourable to the mulberry and, for many months in the year, to the rearing of silkworms. In black Africa and in Madagascar a kind of silk is made from the cocoons of wild butterflies; and in India too there is sericulture. But it is in China that technical developments have advanced furthest. The Far Eastern peoples have never woven wool; and the utilisation of silk was much more difficult. In the countryside of the Yangtse and southeast China many peasants delight in devoting themselves to sericulture, for it is an ideal occupation for those who have little or no land but plenty of time, patience and perseverance (Figs. 8.2 and 8.3).

The mulberries, planted in parallel rows, are not trees, as in Europe, but bushes, cut back each year so as to produce long, leafy shoots that can be plucked by hand. This arrangement has the advantage that the branches do not cast a deep shade on the crops grown in between the mulberry rows. The mulberries will grow on a variety of soils, and their deep roots protect them from short periods of drought. They grow on hillsides, and on the light alluvium of major riverbeds; in the latter situation they may sometimes get flooded, in which case the leaf-harvest is done from light punts made of plaited bamboo; the mulberries will continue to produce new leaves unless they are completely submerged.

In his tiny house the Chinese peasant will set aside a room for the rearing of silkworms. He keeps it as clean as the mud walls and exposed timber framework will allow; he covers the openings with gauze to keep out the blowflies that would lay eggs on the silkworms. He lavishes the most attentive care on the worms, and guards them against all kinds of imaginary external influences: no pregnant woman must enter the cocoonery, not any person returning from a funeral; when a thunderstorm occurs a loud noise is made so that the worms may not be frightened by the thunder. Despite all this solicitude, Chinese sericulture has some serious weaknesses: the worm 'seed' is often badly selected, and hygiene deficient, so that 'pebrine' works havoc among the

Fig. 8.3 Weighing the cocoons (from an eighteenth-century Chinese drawing)

worms. The crisis resulting from low silk prices has struck a serious blow at an activity that was already tottering.

The crisis, indeed, ruined the Japanese sericulture, which was far more scientific than the Chinese. The Japanese silkworm rearer used better worm seed, and his cocooneries were much more hygienic. With government encouragement, sericulture staged a remarkable recovery during the Nipponese revival. The authorities were well aware that silk could bring in considerable revenue without necessitating the purchase of foreign raw materials. More than 2 million peasant families, about one-third of the rural population, were content to devote part of their time to sericulture; and the production of silk trebled in thirty years. The crisis due to the competition of manmade fibres was deeply felt in Japan — but it has been overcome, partly by developing the manufacture of these manmade fibres. Rapid technological progress has enabled Japan to cope with its rising population and at the same time achieve a higher standard of living.

THE POOR DEVELOPMENT OF ANIMAL HUSBANDRY

The Far Eastern peasant is no stock-raiser; he only uses animals as beasts of burden, or for ploughing, with some reluctance, and he consumes but little meat and no milk, butter or cheese; he just doesn't know how to milk a cow. Chickens, ducks, pigs and even dogs are reared for food, but cattle are not kept for the butcher. The Japanese, who were the least carnivorous of the Far Eastern peoples, did not consume, on average, more than 1500 grammes of meat a year. This situation is changing today, at least in the towns (and over one-half of the Japanese population is urban); snack-bars do a great trade in sausages made from whalemeat, Chicago lard and potato starch.

Oxen and buffaloes for ploughing are relatively few in number, and are not employed to capacity; an animal will only work for perhaps fifty or sixty days in a year. It is a common sight to see buffaloes wallowing in the mud while the peasants hoe the fields and carry heavy loads. At a time when tractors had not yet supplanted draught horses in the United States one animal would do four days work for every one day of human labour; in China it was more like half a day of animal labour to one day of human labour (Fig. 8.4).

Animals were used for work that would have needed prolonged human effort, and thus they helped to ease bottlenecks.

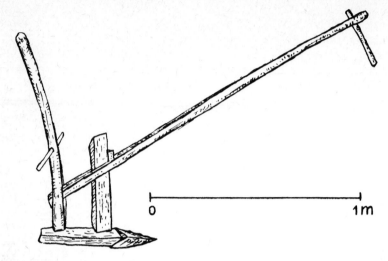

Fig. 8.4 A simple man-operated plough from Shantung (from R. H. Hommel, *China at Work*, N. Y., 1937, 44). The ploughman draws it along by placing his shoulder between the beam and the small piece of wood perpendicular to it. Another man pushes the plough by shoving his shoulder against the upper part of the stilt, whilst with his two hands he presses on the transverse bar in order to keep the plough biting into the soil. The ploughshare has a small iron head

One could sometimes see very poor peasants digging their fields with nothing but a spade, or dragging a harrow across a ricefield, or even perhaps a plough. But normally the peasant would use an animal for ploughing and harrowing; though every other operation would be done by hand. There is, of course, competition for food between animals and man; when the animals are engaged in exceptional physical effort they need exceptional feeding. But the fields in the Far East have nothing to offer to the working animals other than the cereals which the people need for themselves.

The work-animals find' but little pasture; they may graze the sparse herbage of the dykes, or the roadside verges, or cemeteries, and they may wander over deforested and uncultivated hillsides; but here they compete with the people who dig up plants for fuel. During the work season, children are employed to cut tree branches to feed the oxen and buffaloes, who can thus take in nourishment quicker than if they had to find it for themselves:

many hours of human labour to feed one animal for one day. Also, when the animals are working, the peasants may give them rice soup — as wretched a meal as they themselves are consuming. Sometimes, plough-animals will be purchased for the period of ricefield ploughing, and sold again after the harrowing; this gets over the problem of feeding them for the rest of the year.

The Far Eastern countryside contains about one working animal for a little over two hectares of cultivated land. But livestock are very much less numerous than the human population.[1] The peasantries have been able to develop such high population densities because they have relied so little on animals. If the peasants had consumed meat and milk produced by their animals, the rural density could not have been so high. A grass field gives very much less human food, through the medium of grazing animals, than the same surface under a cereal crop. Cattle only convert into weight 6.2 per cent of the dry matter that they consume (57.3 per cent disappears into the atmosphere and 36.5 per cent in excreta); man consumes two-thirds of the animal's weight, so that only $\frac{4}{100}$ of the dry matter consumed by the fat animal is of use to the human being. While one hectare of food crops in China will produce 10 million calories, a hectare of pasture would only give, in the form of milk, 1.7 million calories. It may be estimated that a given quantity of cereals, consumed directly, would feed five times more people than if it were fed to animals and consumed in the form of meat and milk. A diet based on meat and milk is thus a luxury that Far Eastern peasants cannot allow themselves. Far Eastern civilisation, in

[1] For 1935, counting an ox or a horse as one unit, a pig as one-fifth of a unit and a sheep or goat as one-seventh, and ignoring poultry, one arrives at the following figures (with corresponding calculations for 1970—71 in brackets):

Animal units per inhabitant

Japan	0.05	(0.05)	India	0.49	(0.34)
China	0.09	(0.18)	France	0.52	(0.51)
Great Britain	0.29	(0.33)	USA	0.98	(0.67)
Italy	0.33	(0.22)	Australia	5.00	(4.00)
Germany	0.42	(0.31)	Argentina	6.12	(2.57)

excluding cattle-raising, has permitted very high rural population densities that are incompatible with animal-fattening and dairying.

All this had a considerable effect on the rural landscape. Eighty-five per cent of China's cultivated soil was devoted to the production of cereals and pulses for direct human consumption, the remainder being under vegetables, textile fibres and bushy plants. In the United States at the same period (the 1930s), 85 per cent of the farmland produced grass and grain for transformation into meat and milk. Grazing land, unknown in China, occupied 47 per cent of the farmed land in the USA. The farmers of the United States and northwest Europe are concerned with the production of costly foodstuffs, whereas Far Eastern agriculture scratches the soil to produce the basic elements of a vegetarian diet.

It would be inaccurate, and too simple, to explain the low level of stock-raising in the Far East as being due to an economic resignation that conditioned the peasants to the production of the greatest number of food calories for direct human consumption. The contrast is very striking between Chinese civilisation and that of the Mongolian pastoralists on China's northwest frontier. The Chinese have only in a very few local cases come under the influence of these Mongols with whom they have been in contact for thousands of years. Some significant observations could have been made, around 1940, in the Khingan Mountains on the boundary between Manchuria and Mongolia. These are ancient land surfaces which bear the marks of planation at about 1400 m; a moderate enough elevation, but the length and terrible severity of the winters means that the soil remains frozen at depth and is of no use for agriculture. The country was occupied somewhat sparsely, by the Tungus, whose herds of reindeer grazed the lichens that grow on the exposed rock surfaces, and who hunted fur-bearing animals. With the cash obtained from the sale of furs they purchased weapons, tobacco, opium and grain. Then came colonists; from the west, Russians, who occupied the valleys and established pastures for beef cattle and dairy cows; they were reasonably successful, for there was no lack of grass in a summer rain climate and stocks of hay could be amassed for the winter. From the east came the Chinese, attracted by grains of gold dust in the streambeds; to feed the gold-panners the Chinese sowed fields of millet, but with poor results. In this climate, more favourable to grass than to grain, the Russians were armed with better agricultural techniques than the Chinese.

It is remarkable that the mountainous areas within China and Indochina, which would lend themselves to a pastoral economy, are not in fact occupied by prosperous stock-raisers. The mountain peoples, who are ethnically different from those of the plains, do indeed raise a few more cattle than the latter, but they still make no use of milk. The Moi of the Annamese mountains have buffaloes, which they sacrifice (and eat) during festivals, but they do not milk the buffalo cows. The Miao, who live in the higher mountain regions of southern China and Indochina (including Thailand, Laos and Vietnam) take no interest in the milk of their female buffaloes and oxen, though they have large numbers of cattle which they sell and occasionally eat. These cattle browse on the poor pastures that follow forest-cutting; but the Miao prefer to upgrade the pasture and to create reserves of fodder.

Far Eastern civilisation is vegetarian, not of necessity but as a matter of principle. If there is now a necessity, it is not an original trait but has developed subsequently. The much less advanced civilisation of the mountain peoples in southeast Asia, which antedates the penetration of Chinese influences, and in which there is absolutely no restriction on the choice of diet imposed by a high rural population density, still does not contain any diligent or careful pastoral techniques. This lack is one of the most remarkable traits of Far Eastern civilisation; if the peasants had found in their cultural heritage any custom of eating meat and drinking milk, they would not have needed to cluster so thickly on the plains that rural densities now exceed 1000 persons per km^2. The almost exclusively agriculture character of peasant technology and the feeble original development of stock-raising are the causes and not the consequences of high population density.

It is interesting, however, to make some comparison with India; for here is a civilisation very much occupied with pastoralism, using draught animals to a much greater extent than in China, consuming milk and butter with avidity, and still having high rural population densities. High human density can coexist with large numbers of cattle. In India, as in China, the cattle have no meadows to graze, and no reserves of fodder are accumulated.

The Indian diet is no less vegetarian than that of China. Though the Indians relish milk and butter, they really have little of either, except among the wealthier classes. Though they do not eat ox meat, and have feelings of revulsion towards other sorts of meat (while the Chinese will eat as much meat as they can afford), and though they burn dung instead of using it as manure, it cannot be said that Indian civilisation, oriented as it is towards pastoralism, makes better use of animals than the Chinese, which has no such pastoral orientation.

So we are confronted with a paradox: high rural densities in both India and China. In the traditional Chinese civilisation there is no consumption of milk, though meat-eating is not forbidden; there are no meadows, cattle are not sacred, and dung is used as manure. In the traditional Indian civilisation there is avid consumption of milk, which is a much sought-after commodity, often in short supply; meat eating, especially of beef, is strictly forbidden, there are no meadows, the cattle are sacred, and their dung is used as fuel or as a building material. The two civilisations have operated in different ways to produce the same demographic result. It was from the moment of its development as an advanced civilisation that Chinese civilisation took its course. In India, when the rural population was less dense, and grazing grounds were extensive, the cows could satisfy the demand for milk. But the growth of population reduced the grazing areas without reducing the number of cattle, and the milk yield from the undernourished beasts diminished. The two civilisations have developed equally dense rural populations, despite the very different role of cattle; but in both countries no cultivable areas are devoted to grass or to growing fodder crops for the animals.

Far Eastern peasants consume eggs, chickens, pigs and even dogs with great gusto. But the amounts are severely limited by the poverty of the resources. The creatures have no food for themselves, for no human being will give them anything — there is nothing to give. They are not fattened before killing. They are the village scavengers, scratching around in the rubbish dumps (though these are less productive than might be expected, since the peasants carefully place outside their front doors anything that might serve as manure for the fields).

Many peasant families like to raise one pig a year, selling it off when it ceases to grow rapidly. The Chinese pig has a short snout, pointed ears, and a back so curved that the belly almost touches the ground; its rapid growth and small bones have led to its being chosen by English pig-breeders who, by mating Chinese and European breeds, have created new and high-yielding races. But the Chinese pig is very far from wallowing in the abundance enjoyed by his distant English cousin. He grubs around laboriously for his food and is an essential element in the landscape of the village streets. When he is sufficiently fat, he is caught in a large basket, suspended from a bamboo; thus imprisoned, and despite his squeals, he is carried to market by two peasants. Sometimes pig-rearing can become quite a speciality, as in western Chekiang, where Kin Hua was famous for its hams.

Every household has its egg-laying poultry, even though it never feeds them. Ducks and geese are raised in villages that have large enough ponds. A common and attractive sight is a flock of duck, under the care of a herdsman, diving into one pool after another, until, with the approach of evening, he calls them home by rattling a box full of maize seeds, and they dutifully settle themselves inside a small bamboo enclosure. The rearing of poultry led to the development of some very elaborate techniques. The Chinese devised an efficient and practical way of incubating eggs; specialists, using an ingenious device that maintained an even and correct temperature with a minimum expenditure of fuel, hatched out thousands of chicks, especially ducklings, that they then sold to poultry-keepers. The peasants of Sin Feng, in Kwangtung province, keep chickens in narrow and dark cages so that they have no room to move; in this way they obtain birds that are prized for the delicacy of their flesh.

FISHING

Sea-fishing contributes a small mite to the diet of the Chinese peasantry; it is undertaken by specialists, and is of no concern to the vast majority of the peasants. In the countryside, professional fishermen exploit the resources of the rivers and ponds; these fishermen often live on their boats, which are sometimes grouped in floating villages. Such landless villages are administered just like ordinary villages, and they even have their guardian spirit housed in a floating temple. These fisherfolk are also watermen, and derive part of their income from the transport of goods.

One of the most skilled techniques of Chinese fishermen involves the use of cormorants in fishing; after training these birds will dive to catch a fish and bring it back to their master. To prevent them from gobbling up fish of a size that the fisherman would not wish to throw away, they have a ring on the beak. It is said that to ensure the fidelity of their cormorants, the owners will mix a little opium with their feed; dulled by the drug, they will be less tempted to fly away.

Apart from the professional fishermen, most peasants will do a little fishing whenever they can. They even fish their own flooded ricefields; they will spend hours with rod and line, though they rarely catch a sizeable fish. They set fish traps in the ditches, throw casting-nets into the ponds, and manoeuvre large dipnets that are easily withdrawn after immersion thanks to the counterpoise fixed on the end of the lever that supports the frame of the net. They also pull nets that scrape the bottom of the ponds, while children and adolescents go netting for shrimps and crabs, or catch crabs by hand.

Because the fresh waters are much overexploited, the peasants, after hours of toil, will get no more than a few immature fish and some crabs, shrimps and shellfish. However, even these morsels are a welcome addition to the monotonous daily diet. Besides, the peasant could have produced nothing else during the time that he has spent in fishing. Pisciculture offers more certain rewards. It is indeed a form of animal husbandry, depending on a rich store of wisdom and experience. The fish-farmers have acquired an astonishing flair for discovering the precise moment to collect the fish-fry that hatch out along the river banks; the young fish are sold to peasants for stocking their ponds. The Vietnamese fish-fry merchant had developed a strange and complex form of food that enabled the young fish to survive in the waterproof panniers in which they were kept; the excrement of silkworms was steeped in water, and a clay pellet was soaked in this mixture, the pellet afterwards being crumbled into the panniers containing the fish. The merchant walks the countryside with two panniers hanging from a yoke across his shoulders; the continuous shaking helps to keep the water aerated. The peasants throw their purchased fish-fry into the pond, but they know full well that unless they keep them fed they will get little profit out of them. The fish food will comprise rice bran, and excrement of various sorts; ponds fertilised by the outflow of latrines produce an abundance of fish. The fish are here in competition with the pigs that consume the same refuse.

CHAPTER 9

FEEDING THE PEASANTS

To feed a family of five persons, a peasant works like
an animal, but to feed six persons, even a whipped
animal would refuse to work.

Shansi dictum

THE PRINCIPAL FOODSTUFFS

From sheer necessity the peasant will sell his best and most
expensive crops and will himself consume those that are less in
demand. The Tonkin peasant sells his rice and eats sweet potatoes, the north Chinese peasant sells his wheat and eats kaoliang
(it has been calculated that he sold 50 per cent of his wheat
harvest and only 20 per cent of the kaoliang crop). The Korean
peasant sold the rice that he grew and purchased cheap Man-
churian millet, which was less expensive than wheat. As the
peasants are well aware, sweet potatoes, millet and kaoliang are
less digestible than wheat; but for this very reason they occupy
the stomach for a longer time and stave off the pangs of
hunger.

Japanese peasants used to eat more barley, sweet potatoes and
millet than rice, which was a luxury food, to be used for feasts
and for sick people. 'Is he ill enough to be given rice?', one
peasant would say to another, speaking of a sick person whose
condition seemed to be deteriorating. Tea, for most peasants, was
also a luxury, and for many was drunk only on great occasions.

The diet of the Far Eastern peasant, essentially vegetarian, is
made up chiefly of cereals, with a much smaller quantity of
tubers. Rich in carbohydrates, these products occupied a more
important place than the bread, alimentary pastes and potatoes

in Western diets. In Honan in 1930 rice comprised 78 per cent by weight of the peasant's diet; sweet potatoes (13 per cent) and some small quantities of other cereals brought up to 95 per cent the share of cereals and tubers; other types of food were of negligible importance. In China's northern provinces, wheat, millet, kaoliang and maize took the place of rice. In Shantung, sweet potatoes were rather more important at 21 per cent of the total food intake by weight. By 1930 the ordinary (or 'Irish') potato had risen to a place of importance in the regions of more continental climate (in Shansi, 10 per cent, and even 21 per cent in Suiyuan). Other Far Eastern diets were of the same general kind, dominated by cereals and tubers. The part played by potatoes must surely increase, for this crop was late in being introduced into peasant culture. As a hoed-up cleaning crop the potato fits admirably into the agricultural pattern. Sugar consumption was almost nil; in the countryside, it was known only in the form of sweets sold by itinerant traders.

In China the pulses, including various sorts of peas and beans, and especially soya, take second place in the diet. These items add to the small quantities of protein and fats that are contained in the cereals. Animal protein and fat are consumed in only minute amounts. The vegetarian diet of the Far Eastern peasant thus depends almost exclusively on cereals and pulses. Green vegetables and fruit (except in Japan) figure in tiny quantities only. Chinese peasants grow but few green vegetables; they prefer to devote all their land and all their available manure to the cereal crops.

Milk, butter and cheese play no part at all in the diet. The Chinese appear to have a positive revulsion for these products; it is a peasant belief that whoever drinks cow's milk establishes a degrading relationship between himself and the cow. Neither does the Chinese peasant eat any quantity of beef or mutton. Pork and poultry may be eaten on feast days — but such days are not as numerous as in Europe. Freshwater fish are scarce, and as for sea fish, their price puts them out of reach of the peasants.

All these facts can be simply expressed in terms of the percentage of the calorie intake derived from each of the major types of food; a comparison with the United States pinpoints the utter lack of balance in the Chinese situation:

118   *Feeding the peasants*

Percentage of total calories available in food[1]

Food group	China	USA
Cereals and pulses	91.8	38.2
Vegetables and roots	5.2	9.0
Sugar	0.5	10.1
Fruit	0.2	3.0
Animal products	2.3	39.2

[1] From J. L. Buck, *Land Utilization in China*, 1937, p. 414.

The low consumption of animal products is, of course, related to the population density, for a hectare of cereals yields more calories than a hectare of grass, or than the harvest of a hectare of cereals transformed into meat and milk. It is also true that the low consumption of animal products results from the poverty of the peasants, because one calorie of animal origin costs more than a vegetable calorie. But, as we have seen, the vegetarian diet is of very ancient origin, and it was a characteristic of the civilisation before it became an inevitable consequence of population density and poverty. However, it may well be that in the Far East as a whole the vegetarian diet derives in part from a respect for animal life, reinforced by the philosophy of Buddhism. Buddhism was not an original cause, for the characteristic diet was already there before the introduction of this religion; and the mountain people, who are not Buddhist, are almost as completely vegetarian as the populations of the plains.

A strong vegetarian tendency appeared quite early, as evidenced by Chinese philosophers: Mencius (third century BC) considered it cruel to kill animals and eat their flesh; however, he may not have practised what he preached, for, as he himself said 'a man of quality never goes near the kitchen'. Certainly, Buddhist influence discouraged the killing of animals, and to abstain from meat was a means of acquiring merit. Even in 1933, after a great flood, the authorities of Hankow (now included in Wuhan) forbade the sale of meat for three days, to atone for the sins of the people and to calm the raging torrent. It is not considered cruel, however, to drink milk; and if the Far Eastern peasant ignores milk, butter and cheese, it is not from religious scruples, but simply from ancient traditions, lack of technical knowhow, and economic necessity.

DIETARY REGIMES

The diets of various regions in the Far East exhibit many variations, even though the main theme is always the same. In the plains of Shantung, Chihli, Shensi and Kansu, the diet is extremely monotonous, and very poor in meat, fish, green vegetables and fruit. In southern China there is more pork and more fresh vegetables. The Vietnamese peasant consumes even more pork and also vegetables and fish; he tries to have a little fish sauce (*nuoc mam*) with every meal. This fish sauce is the product of the autodigestion of the fish by its own digestive juices; it is effected in a pickle that is strong enough to prevent putrefaction and weak enough for the digestion to take place. The result is a liquid rich in high-quality protein, and easily assimilable. The Vietnamian *nuoc mam* is one of the numerous sauces and fish or shrimp pastes that are prepared in southeast Asia. In Vietnam, it is a survival from the pre-Chinese era, as also is the chewing of areca nuts and betel leaves. The Chinese have no taste for either *nuoc mam* or the mastication of areca and betel (though betel chewing was shown on the 'battle of flowers' in Canton in the eighteenth century); their sauces have a soya base.

The Japanese consume more vegetables than the Chinese: fresh vegetables, or preserved in pickle or vinegar. *Takuwan-zake* is made from slices of daikon, the Japanese giant radish, with rice bran and salt; *umeboshi* is made from plums. Bowls of rice are most commonly accompanied by *shoyu*, a soya sauce, or *miso*, a sauce made from wheat, beans and salt. The carefully-managed narrow terraces on the hillslopes produce vegetables in association with mulberries and fruit trees.

Japan also makes great use of sea-food. The Japanese fishing industry was the world's largest, in terms of tonnage caught, until it lost its supremacy to the fisheries of Peru. But the Peruvian catch is of much lower value, consisting as it does mainly of anchovies destined for conversion into fishmeal. Japanese seafood is more varied and more valuable. Seaweed, cultivated on thousands of hectares, is consumed in greater quantity than meat. The rising standard of life allows the Japanese people to buy more expensive fish, the product of advanced and costly technology. Japanese fishing craft seek tuna from as far afield as the coasts of West Africa, transporting it back to Japan.

The poverty of the Far Eastern diet in protein and fats, particularly those of animal origin, explains the eagerness to fish the freshwater ponds and the rivers; and the readiness of the peasants to eat insects. The Tonkin peasants eat silkworms, water-bugs that give the *nuoc mam* the taste of a sour apple, locusts, crickets, mole crickets, grasshoppers, mayflies, bee larvae, ants' eggs, caterpillars, mudworms (palolo) and snails.

THE LOW COST OF FOOD

The diet is normally monotonous and tasteless. In Kiangsu, about 1930, a family of peasant proprietors (and not on the lowest economic level) would usually have three meals a day; the first would be rice soup, prepared with plenty of water, a little rice and a few dried vegetables; the second, more substantial, would consist of rather more rice, together with 'cabbage' leaves (the 'Chinese cabbage' is a plant of the mustard family); the third meal was again rice soup, prepared by boiling up the rice left over from the previous meal. No dessert; and fruit a delicacy consumed only between meals.

This was hardly a substantial diet; so, at times of intense labour — planting-out or harvest — the better-off families of Kiangsu would have five meals a day. The first would be sticky rice with sugar, the second, rice soup and stale vegetables, the third rice with green vegetables, the fourth, the most important, rice with vegetables, some meat, and alcoholic drink, and the fifth, served very late, rice with more stale vegetables. During periods of inactivity, the poorest peasants, who had no stocks of food, went into a kind of enforced hibernation, sleeping for long periods in order to eat as little as possible; they seldom had more than one meal a day. In times of famine, the tiny stocks put aside for just such an occasion would be brought out, and the meal would consist of soup made from wild herbs, with a few pinches of flour or a few grains of rice.

In accordance with the general level of poverty, food was very cheap. There was not another country in the world in which it was possible to feed so inexpensively. A peasant in the Red River delta, in 1934, could quell his hunger for one day for no more than 4 cents, the equivalent of 40 centimes in France. The 500 grammes of polished rice that he consumed in a day cost no more than 2 cents (20 centimes), and the rest would be spent on complementary (and in the peasant's view, secondary) items. In China, at the same period, prices were slightly higher than the exceptionally low Tonkin levels, and a peasant would spend about 20 French francs a month on food. In Japan prices were a little higher still.

Despite the modest level of their resources and the poverty of their diet, the Far Eastern peasants did not abstain entirely from the consumption of items that have little or no food value. Like other people, they smoke and drink alcoholic liquors. Both the peasant and his wife take frequent puffs at a waterpipe; he takes his pipe to the fields, and relaxes from his labours by filling his lungs with smoke that has been cooled in bubbling through the water. Alcohol is not a regular drink: it comes out only on great occasions such as anniversary feasts, weddings or funerals. One never sees a drunken peasant, for their total consumption is only one or two litres of rice alcohol in a whole year. The use of opium is not widespread in the countryside; only a few old people, to whom nothing is refused out of respect for their great age, are allowed to smoke it.

In normal times, that is when there are no shortages or actual famine, the peasant diet is adequate in calories but deficient in protein and fat, especially of animal origin. The fear of want constantly occupies the mind of the peasant, and this certainly does not reflect a life of plenty. 'Have you eaten?' is the polite greeting between two Chinese peasants. One never sees fat people in the villages, nor even an individual with a tendency to stoutness. Ceremonies, whether family, religious or communal, are accompanied by feasts, where everyone present enjoys large helpings and dishes that rise above the ordinary monotonous level. In China, a married daughter visiting her parents would expect them to lay on a large feast at their own expense, and would take away as much food as possible, even though it left their cupboards bare; and she would take her children too, so that the spoils from the visit could be more fruitful. Such visits were regarded by the brothers remaining at home, and even more by their wives, as catastrophes, the more unbearable since there was no redress, for they could have no pretext for conducting a reprisal raid on their sister. From such visits arose disputes of epic proportions that aroused much interest in the neighbourhood.

It is noteworthy that the poor diet and often insufficient food intake of the Far Eastern peasants has not led to any hereditary degeneracy. The people live and multiply, retaining all their physical and intellectual qualities, despite their poor nourishment and low standards of hygiene. It is true that an improvement in the nourishment of children leads, as has been seen in Japan, to a notable increase in the stature of adults. The hereditary potential of growth has not been attained over the centuries because of deficient diet.

FUEL SUPPLIES

The peasants are faced with a fuel problem — fuel for cooking, fuel for heating. The problem is least apparent in those parts where there is no real winter, as in Vietnam and southeast China. But in northern China and northern Japan, the winter cold is severe. How this is reflected in house construction will be dealt with in Chapter 14.

At all events, even where there is no need for winter heating, fuel is a rarity. There is no question of buying it; it must be gathered where it can be found, at no monetary expense. So rice is cooked only once a day, to save both time and fuel. Brushwood and straw are the main fuels, and much time must be spent in cooking, for the pot cannot be left for long in case the fire goes out. The peasant will even hesitate to boil water for tea-making. If a log remains unburnt when the rice is cooked, it will be plunged into water so that it can be used again and does not burn unnecessarily. The success of a fresh dish depends on the rapidity of its cooking, and they like quick-cooked food. They say that 'what one puts under the kettle is of more value than what one puts inside it'.

The scarcity of fuel is easily explained: the plains are entirely cultivated, and where there are no adjacent brush-covered hills, the only resources available to the peasant are the straw and haulms of plants, and roots. After the harvest, the peasant returns to his field with a large rake to collect up the remaining straw. But this process is unfortunate for soil fertility, because it deprives the soil of every scrap of organic matter.

Chinese peasants living on the fringe of hilly areas first cut firewood, then destroyed the forest, and finally denuded the hillsides of bushes. It has needed the establishment of a strong and much-feared authority to initiate reafforestation projects and to have them respected.

CHAPTER 10

PEASANT INDUSTRY AND TRADE

Bits of bamboo and fragments of wood are always useful.

Chinese proverb

He who would enrich himself should remember that agriculture is worth less than craftsmanship, and the latter is worth less than commerce. Embroidery won't bring in as great an income as a meat-stall in the market.

Chinese saying of the Han period (1st century BC)

Peasant production is the 'root' of the economy, and craft industries and commercial activities are the 'small branches of the tree'. This was the traditional Chinese view of their economy. But a Tonkin peasant was only occupied in his fields for about 125 days a year, a Chinese peasant for 120 and a Korean peasant for 140 days; Japanese figures were of the same order. The peasants thus had ample time at their disposal and so could engage in industry and trade, both of which helped to augment their meagre income.

PEASANT INDUSTRIES

During their unoccupied time the peasants could make objects for sale. The village crafts that thus developed took on a number of interesting characteristics that were not inevitable but reflected certain peculiarities of the traditional economy. In the first place, there was the tendency for technical specialisation. Of course, every peasant, man and woman, had mastered certain simple techniques; they could all make baskets from bamboo, and could sew and darn. But once the technique reached a certain degree of complexity it became the province of specialists. These specialists were not to be found in every village: all villages did not have a shoemaker, a potter, a blacksmith, a coppersmith or a hairdresser. On the other hand there were some villages in which all the men were engaged in some speciality. As a result, village specialists went round to other villages offering services that the local inhabitants could not provide.

Specialisation could be carried to great lengths, such as making only semifinished articles and selling them to another village for completion; or in utilising only part of the purchased raw material and selling the remainder on account. The makers of straw hats from palm leaves, for example, used only part of the leaves, selling off the residue to the makers of raincoats.

It is usually quite impossible to explain the localisation of an industry in this or that village as being due to any local advantages of situation or the availability of local raw material (Fig. 10.1). Why should a particular village in Anhwei make felt slippers, or a Japanese village specialise in lacquered ware, or a Tonkin village produce coats made of leaves, while neighbouring villages have a quite different industry or none at all? Many villages must transport their raw materials over inadequate footpaths, whereas the industry could just as well have been located not far away, on the banks of a river in much more propitious circumstances. A village of silk-spinners would get its cocoons from another village, and this one in turn might get its mulberry leaves from a third village. It would appear that an industry, once having been established without any particular local economic advantages, maintained itself without suffering competitive economic selection. How was this possible? At first the craftsmen had no machines, using only the strength and agility of their hands. They thus had no need to locate themselves near to sources of power. Further, they were content to work immensely hard for but trivial gains. They sold their finished articles at little more than the cost of the raw material, and an hour's labour was

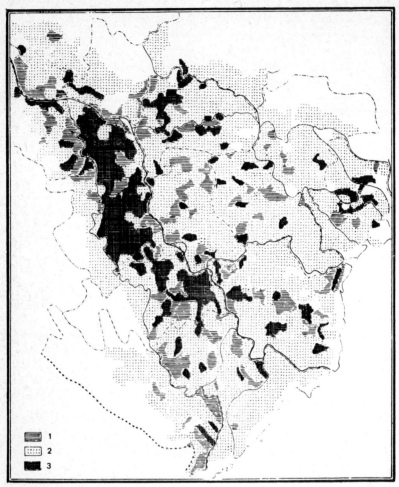

Fig. 10.1 Artisan population of the Red River delta in 1936. The map shows that most of the craftsmen were to be found in the northwestern part of the delta, near to the city of Hanoi, where their wares were most in demand. Scale 1/1M.
Key: 1. average density of artisan population (4 to 6 per 100 inhabitants); 2. small artisan population (under 4 per 100); 3. large artisan population (more than 6 per 100 inhabitants)

extremely badly rewarded. The low standard of living made these very low profits both possible and necessary, and they were permissible only because they represented 'pin-money', the peasants remaining primarily agriculturalists. The making of reed-baskets would not yield an income of more than 50 centimes a day for a Tonkin Delta family in 1935; despite their low level of demand they could not possibly have subsisted on this — but of course their rice and other crops provided their main resource.

The apparently irrational localisations are thus explained. When a certain craft is deeply rooted in a village, the peasants seek to create a monopoly by carefully guarding their special 'tricks of the trade'. One example of this has already been given — the village that holds and preserves the secret of the reproduction of the 'azolla' pond weed. The same monopolistic tendency is seen in the villages that control transport on certain lengths of river. The Chinese have always been very reluctant to divulge their techniques; tradition has it that Vietnamians travelling through China adopted many ruses to discover some of them; and thanks to this industrial espionage, most of the village industries of Tonkin derive from Chinese peasant crafts, in particular, the techniques of forging and other metal-working, of dyeing, spinning and weaving.

Industrial operations, like those of agriculture, were characterised by the immense expenditure of labour and the subtlety of the methods. Dyeing, the making of rice-sugar (we should call it 'barley-sugar'), pottery, to take but three examples, showed a variety of skilful and efficient techniques. But always the work involved was enormous. In a village of dyers, the production of black silk required ten successive cycles of the following operations: boiling in the dye-bath (the heating of which was a very slow and inconvenient procedure), the dye itself being prepared from various materials including the leaves of a species of *Terminalia*, steeping in a special mud having fixative properties, washing in the water of a pond that had special qualities, and finally drying. Ten repetitions of four processes, or forty operations in all, each one of which is in itself complex (as for example the boiling of the dye-bath, involving fetching the water, carrying the fuel, keeping the fire going, preparing the materials and stirring the silk in the bath). The result of it all was a very remarkable product, but the earnings were extremely low.

The artisans worked with nimbleness and accuracy; indeed to

watch the speed and dexterity of some of them almost made one dizzy. The making of 'gold and silver bars' to be burnt at altars in Tonkin is an example. Their framework is a thin leaf of bamboo, folded into four; around this is wound a strip of paper, white to represent silver bars, yellow for gold. The result looks rather like a matchbox. A skilled worker could make 3000 of these in a day, repeating 3000 times the two operations just described; but previous to this he would have had to transport the bamboo and cut it to the appropriate size, buy the paper from the specialist makers, colour it, cut it into the required lengths and make the strips.

Another example of the delicacy of Chinese peasant craftsmanship is to be found in the highly ingenious method of alcoholic fermentation by the action of certain yeasts on cereals. In fact the operation adds to the yeast no less than twenty-eight ingredients, the analysis of which has shown that they are very useful in hindering the development of micro-organisms that have a bad influence on fermentation and on the contrary hasten the desired process.

Village industries were still very much alive in 1940. Some, of course, had disappeared, that were concerned with articles no longer in use, such as certain ornaments, old-fashioned hats, palanquins, and bamboo parasols. Others were already suffering the competition of factory products, like the spinning and weaving of cotton. In Japan the domestic cotton industry had already succumbed, as had the domestic preparation of tea, tobacco, soya sauce, mustard oil, paper, and polished rice. Many new rural crafts had spread, but they did not compensate for the losses. In China and in Tonkin rural industries were more resistant, thanks to the lower standard of life and the weaker development of modern industries. But this was only a respite; there is no future for village crafts. Already efforts have been made in communist

---

Fig. 10.2   **The preparation of sea-salt, on the island of Tsong Ming in the Yangtsé delta (from an illustration in P. H. Havret, *L'Ile de Tsong Ming; variétés sinologiques No. 1.*, Shanghai, 1892; the drawing itself is taken from the 1760 edition of the *Chronicles of the Tsong Ming subprefecture*). The salt is obtained by the evaporation of brine (that has already been concentrated by exposure to the air in tanks) in cauldrons over a furnace fuelled by reeds**

China to establish in the people's communes small and partly
mechanised factories that produced beyond the needs of the
locality and sold tools or pottery outside. After thousands of
years, however, village industries are still not quite dead.

PEASANT TRADE

The most elementary form of commerce was the rural market,
where peasants of both sexes assembled to buy and sell, to gossip
and to hear news of the world outside. Anyone with a few coins
to spare could eat food unobtainable in his village — such as dog
sausages, beef soup, and fresh noodles. Villages did not welcome
markets within their enclosures, for fear of the disorders that
might follow from the intrusion of 'foreign' merchants; so the
markets were set up in the open country, at the meeting place of
paths. The transactions would be of very small value, no more
than a few cents of a piastre or Chinese dollar.

These markets also attracted professional traders, such as cloth
merchants, sellers of medicines, caterers, hairdressers (who also
practised the rather alarming curetting of eyes and ears with
small copper instruments). These professional traders usually
came from villages that specialised in trading activities, but their
supplies — of cloth for example — came from the small wholesalers in the towns. Itinerant traders went from village to village
buying up hair and horn and selling to the wholesalers. The
professional merchants used 'chinese' scales (the 'steelyard', first
used in the Mediterranean area in the first century BC and taken
to China by Syrian merchants).

The transport of merchandise required large amounts of
human labour, for there were almost no roads accessible to carts
or motorised vehicles; and it must be remembered that draught
animals were in competition with human porters for the consumption of cereals. In Szechwan, in 1938, the cost of coal transport in panniers suspended from a yoke doubled the pithead
price after a journey of only 20 km. In the whole of China, in
1938, the price of a tonne-kilometre of human porterage was
about 0.62 Chinese dollars, or 6 or 7 French francs of that

period.[1] The human porter was poorly paid, for he only earned the equivalent of 5 French francs for carrying 40 kg over 30 km in a day. However, even at these very low rates the cost of transport was crippling, being ten or twenty times higher than by modern methods. It was impossible, under such conditions, to carry heavy loads for long distances; 100 km was about the limit. When shortages or actual famine affected large areas, creating a huge demand for the movement of foodstuffs, it was impossible to supply the needs without water transport. The provisioning of Chinese armies operating far from their bases created great problems for the administration, as Su Ma Tsien clearly demonstrated.

[1] Value of Chinese dollar in early 1930s:

1929 100 Chinese dollars equalled 41.51 US dollars
1930 100 Chinese dollars equalled 29.90 US dollars
1931 100 Chinese dollars equalled 22.14 US dollars
1932 100 Chinese dollars equalled 21.49 US dollars
1933 100 Chinese dollars equalled 26.05 US dollars
1934 100 Chinese dollars equalled 33.91 US dollars

CHAPTER 11

PEASANT POVERTY

More honest men will be found in the prisons than in the custom-houses.

Mandarins within sight of money are like leeches seeing blood.

Chinese proverbs

NORMAL EXPENDITURE

In Tonkin, a relatively well-to-do peasant family of five persons spent about 50 piastres a year in 1935, equivalent to about 500 French francs, and consumed 1500 kg of rice valued at about 60 piastres. This family thus lived on the equivalent of 90 francs a month, or 3 francs a day; and food represented 72 per cent of the total expenditure (including their own produce). Direct taxation amounted to 10 piastres, or 9 per cent of the total expenses, and clothing cost a little more than this; feasts, anniversaries, and the expenses associated with religious worship absorbed another 12 per cent. The income barely equalled the expenditure. It included 32 piastres (42 per cent of the total monetary income) from the sale of rice, 8 piastres (10 per cent) from the sale of vegetables, fruit and dried products, 14 piastres (18 per cent) from animal products, 6 piastres (8 per cent) from crafts and trading, and 11 piastres (14 per cent) from wages. Rice, either consumed or sold, constituted 67 per cent of the total income (not merely the monetary income) of this relatively prosperous family, owners of one hectare of good agricultural land.

The total expenses of a family of Korean peasants (including their own produce) was barely 210 yen a year in 1930, and this sum was hardly equalled by their income. The cost of food and fuel amounted to 72 per cent of the total outgoings, and the average daily expenditure of one person was the ridiculously small sum of 0.116 yen. This extremely low standard of living was falling even lower, for the Japanese were occupying more and more land. If Japanese farmers actually established themselves on the land, it was lost to the Koreans; if they allowed the Koreans to remain as tenant farmers, they squeezed a large part of the harvest out of them. One serious indication of the falling standard of living of the Korean peasant was given by the diminution in rice consumption, which fell from 120 litres a year per person in 1912 to 83 litres in 1930 — during which time the consumption in Japan increased from 193 to 204 litres. This was accompanied also by an increase in the amount of millet consumed, from 46 to 63 litres; and millet, though cheaper, was much less appreciated.

The standard of living of the Chinese peasants, everywhere modest, varied from region to region; it was generally lower in the north than in the south. In 1925 the average annual expenditure of a Chinese peasant family in the north, numbering six persons, did not exceed 190 Chinese dollars; in the Yangtse delta, the figure rose to 290 dollars. The difference was slightly reduced because the cost of living was somewhat higher in central China; but it corresponded to a slight inequality in the degree of poverty, for whereas in the north food represented 62 per cent of the total expenditure, this percentage was a little lower in the Yangtse plain. Expenditure on less essential or even non-essential items was more important in Kiangsu and Fukien than in northern China: clothing, 8.6 per cent as against 6.4 in the north (where however the climate was colder); education, religion and festivals, 11.5 per cent as against 7.3; amusements 6.2 against 2.9. The difference in the standard of living of these two parts of China was excellently demonstrated in certain cantons of Kiangsu. Here, peasants from Shantung, driven from their homeland by sheer misery, had occupied vacant hill lands that the native people of Kiangsu had neglected. Eventually, despite their poverty and by dint of much parsimony, these people from Shantung were able to buy plots of land on the plain, and so oust some of the 'natives'. The Kiangsu people never accepted the immigrants into their family circles, and the slight differences in customs were resented by these juxtaposed peasants.

Averages can be misleading. Millions of Chinese peasants were below the mean, in terms of living standards. Almost incredibly low standards existed in parts of the north; even in the vicinity of Peking, in 1922, a large percentage of families lived on less than 50 Chinese dollars a year, or the equivalent at that time of 250 French francs or 25 American dollars. The problem can be looked at from another angle: if each peasant needed, for adequate sustenance, 0.18 hectare of cultivated land, and if each family comprised five or six persons, a rural holding should have been about one hectare in size; but in fact one-third of the holdings in rural China were less than 0.60 hectare.

While the average expenditure of a peasant family in northern China in 1925 amounted to 190 Chinese dollars (or US $95), that of an American family, numbering fewer persons, was 2960 Chinese dollars (US $1480); in fact the annual budget of an American farmer was almost twenty times larger than that of the Chinese peasant. It is difficult for anyone in the West to understand how a Chinese could live for a whole year on the equivalent of 16 American dollars, or a Korean on 42 yens (in 1930, equal to about 17 American dollars of 1924), or a Tonkinois on 22 piastres in 1934 (equal to about 16—18 American dollars of 1924). Of course it is difficult to make direct monetary comparisons, and perhaps the value of housing is underestimated; but it is perfectly clear that these Far Eastern peasants had extremely scanty resources.

FARM RENTS

The peasants of eastern Asia cultivate very small plots of land, and what is more, they do not reap the whole benefit of their labours. Their already tiny income is further reduced by rents, taxes, disasters, usury, and bad sales organisation.

Twelve per cent of the cultivated lands in northern China were rented, 40 per cent in central and south China. Usually the lessees gave half the revenue to the landowner and themselves bore all the expenses except the land tax — that is, fertilisers, implements, animals, labour, and seed. Moreover they were under an obligation to make substantial gifts to the landowner several times a year.

The conditions under which the tenant farmers operated were thus severe. Even so however the proprietor would only get a yield on his real-estate capital of about 8 per cent per annum, and this was not excessive in a country where the usual rate for money on loan was 20 or 30 per cent. It was the price of land that accounted for the relatively low return obtained by the non-farming landowner, despite the onerous rental arrangements.

The rental conditions varied according to the density of population, being most severe in the densest areas, and according to local custom. They were not particularly onerous in Kiangsu and Kwangtung; and in Chekiang the lessee actually possessed the land, and could not be ejected if he continued to pay his rent; he could sublet, sell it and bequeath it as a heritage, and the cost of permanent improvements would be divided between the lessee and the lessor.

On the whole, relations between tenant farmers and land-owners were stable and courteous; the tenants usually remained all their lives on the same plot, for they were very conscious of the relevance of the Kiangsu proverb — 'By the departure of a tenant farmer the tenant himself, the proprietor and the land are all made poorer.' It was the custom for friendly meetings to be arranged between the tenant and the landowner, always enlivened by a meal, the indispensable accompaniment of every Chinese encounter. When the threshing of the grain was finished, the tenant invited the proprietor to a feast, after which the harvest was divided. For his part the proprietor returned the compliment by offering the tenant a banquet when the grain was delivered.

In Kiangsu, when a tenant wished to quit his farm he raised the sails of the windmill on the day the proprietor came to share out the harvest. By this sign the proprietor would know the intentions of his tenant without any word being spoken between them that might have been either inappropriate or foolish. 'Face' was saved on both sides, and tenant and proprietor met with the usual ceremony, as if nothing of importance was about to affect their relations.

The tenant farmers exercised their ingenuity to deceive the landowner by concealing part of the harvest; if the owner was represented by an agent or steward, the tenant would purchase the latter's complicity. But all too often the stewards aggravated the poverty of the peasants by extorting contributions and 'presents' under threat of eviction. All this did not take place without complaints, agitation and even violence. The tenant farmers of the Shanghai region became so tired of the constant confrontations that they handed over the administration of their affairs to specialist agents who managed groups of neighbouring properties. As a result there was no longer any direct link between the landowner and his land; the Shanghai capitalist invested in real estate, but left its management to an agent.

In Japan in 1938 there were about 5 600 000 rural landholdings, of which 1 740 000 were owner-occupied, 1 500 000 were rented and 2 370 000 of mixed character (holdings that the farmer partly owned and partly rented). The tenant farmers were sharecroppers who retained one-half of the harvest for themselves; but their income was reduced by the expenses that they were obliged to incur, for fertilisers, seeds and so on. In monetary terms, the sharecropper only benefited from about one-quarter of his 'raw' harvest. The sharecroppers were a stable community, with a father-to-son inheritance. The landowners tended to regard 'their' sharecroppers as clients, over whom they exercised some rights. Thus the landowner would recruit from the sharecropper families his domestic servants and factory workers, for it often happened that the landowners also ran small industries; the landowner could also extract a premium from larger industrialists for providing them with workers, and so could in fact act as a privileged usurer for his sharecroppers.

The traditional peasant resignedness did not prevent numerous clashes. In 1934, for example, there were some 6000 confrontations involving no less than 120 000 sharecroppers, about 5 per cent of the then total numbers. The tenants formed associations to promote their claims for the prevention of arbitrary and uncompensated evictions and the lowering of rents. Passive resistance and rent strikes were their weapons. The reforms of 1946, as we shall see, transformed the whole agrarian situation; however, the considerable changes in the rural landscape have been

due, not so much to the reforms as to the extraordinary economic expansion of Japan.

In Tonkin, as noted above, village solidarity prevented the
tenants from being tied hands and feet by the cupidity of the
landowners. In general, the sharecropper paid his rent not as cash
but as a proportion of the harvest, and in practice the amount
varied with the density of population and the fertility of the soil.
In densely populated districts, with rich soils, the landowner
might take the whole of the paddy harvest, leaving the tenant
with nothing but the dry-season crops. But there were also, in
Tonkin, tenant farmers who paid a fixed rent, either in cash or in
kind. As elsewhere, both the sharecroppers and the tenant
farmers had their outgoings increased by the 'presents' they were
obliged to give to the landowner, in the form of sugar, poultry,
fruit, at the time of major festivals. Further, they had to give
some days of unpaid labour to the landowner (during which
time, however, they were fed at the latter's expense).

In general, when the harvest was poor, the landowner agreed
to a reduction of the rent; but a stubborn landowner would
demand the acknowledgement of a debt, and this set the tenant
on a perilous path. It was virtually impossible for the tenant to
repay the debt, swollen by a high rate of interest. He might, if he
owned a small plot of land, mortgage this to the landowner to
cover the debt; but such an arrangement might provoke many
and costly legal proceedings. 'To win a law suit is to gain a cat
and lose a cow', said a Chinese proverb. But the fondness for
litigation might outweigh the justifiable fears, and a wise peasant
might find himself dragged before a tribunal in his own defence
against a dishonest neighbour.

TAXES

Direct taxes were not graduated, the capitation tax was fixed,
and land tax was simply proportional to the extent of the land
held. The peasants preferred the principle of direct taxation.
Before 1939, in Japan, a rural landholding on which the gross
income was 570 yens paid a direct tax of 58 yens. In China the

peasants were heavily taxed. Only the financial ill-will of the country-dwellers prevented the authorities from being even more grasping. About 1934, in certain provinces, the land taxes had been paid several dozen years in advance. The authorities had discovered an ingenious means of reconciling their official hostility to opium and their real desire to retain the great profits from the illicit drug traffic: the owners of poppyfields had imposed on them not a tax but a heavy fine, which however still left the cultivator with a substantial profit. The fine was imposed annually, just like a tax, and the peasants were thus in effect incited to sow more poppies, which alone would allow them to pay the fine. The troubles that so enfeebled China in the first half of the twentieth century hit the peasants very hard, for they were subject to a multitude of requisitions and forced contributions levied by the plundering armies of the various military potentates under whom the country was suffering. In 1928, for example, the people of a district of Kiangsu lost about one-twentieth of their income through the arbitrary taxes, requisitions and pillaging of the army; this was a disaster for so inflexible a budget as that of the Chinese peasant. In other areas there were insurrections and massacres as well; bands of Muslim Dungans killed hundreds of thousands of peasants in Kansu and Shensi. The Tai Ping revolt, in the middle of the twentieth century, resulted in 20 million deaths in central China.

DISASTERS

Northern China is exposed to droughts that increase in severity towards the northwest, approaching the Great Wall. Suspecting the onset of a drought, the peasants make great efforts to counteract it by watering the most accessible parts of their fields. But a pitiless sun shining from a completely cloudless sky offers them no assistance. The prospect of a poor harvest sends up the price of food well before the expected arrival of the monsoon, and the poorest people, with no stocks to fall back on pending the next harvest, soon begin to suffer cruelly. Then the monsoon yields but a small harvest of rain and grain, and the larder is almost empty. There are shortages, and then real famine. Lack of adequate and efficient transport made it impossible to transport the quantities of food necessary to sustain millions of hungry stomachs. And help would need to be sought from far afield, for the neighbouring provinces, also more or less affected by drought, had no surpluses to offer.

Panic seized the population. They fled, devouring wayside herbs and roots, however unpalatable; some sold all their possessions to buy food; they even sold their wives and children to save them from starving to death. Hordes descended on the towns, leaving a trail of dead and dying behind them; for the towns were less completely devoid of supplies. Here is a pathetic example of Chinese peasant ingenuity: as if he were about to make a purchase, a man would handle a roasted duck in order to soak his fingers in the juice, then, dividing his rice into ten small portions, he would suck each finger in turn as he ate the mouthfuls of rice. The famished people might find in the town some assistance from the authorities or charitable institutions, who might organise soup kitchens; or they could beg amongst the townsfolk for burnt rice stuck to the bottom of the cooking pots.

At the first fall of rain those who had fled would return to their ancestral homes and resume the precarious exploitation of the soil. The most difficult part was to find seed (and to refrain from eating it before sowing it!) The survivors of such an ordeal would have vivid recollections of it, which they would pass on to their children with instructions as to what to do if famine should strike again. Such instructions would include details of wild seeds, plants and roots that might be eaten. Chou Ting Wang, the fifth son of the founder of the Ming dynasty, actually wrote a book, published in 1406, entitled *Herbs for the Prevention of Famine*.

Floods can produce disasters even more appalling than droughts. Droughts simply destroy the crop that is growing, but floods scour the land, destroy food stocks, and drown the inhabitants. The mud-built house walls collapse, and the destruction of the granaries ruins both food supplies and seed grain.

Recovery from such disasters is very difficult, for the poor peasants have lost their draught animals and their stores of seed, and cannot regain the rhythm of their agricultural operations after the waters have receded. But somehow they manage it, and after several months of sheer hard labour, the boundaries of their holdings are uncovered from beneath the alluvial mud, the fields are recultivated, temporary shelters are built, such house frame-works as have not been washed away are re-erected, and the ancestral graves stripped of their cover of silt.

Changes through the ages in the course of the distributaries in the Yellow River delta, which extends 800 km from the northernmost to the southernmost arm, have ruined tens of millions of Chinese peasants. In 1931 the floods of the Yangtse and its tributaries devastated 160 000 km² and drowned 140 000 people; the number of those who died of starvation was never determined, but at least 25 million people must have been affected in some way by this catastrophe; some 40 per cent of these were forced to evacuate from August until the following March. More than half of all the houses in the area were des-troyed. The total loss was estimated at 2000 million Chinese dollars (about 10 000 million French francs at that period); a very formidable sum in a country where the total income of a family was under 300 dollars a year. But the disaster made imperative the development of a rational system of carefully maintained dykes.

The great famine of 1849 resulted in 14 million deaths; that of 1878—79 killed somewhere between 9 and 13 million. Between 1926 and 1946 Kansu province, ravaged by drought and by the consequences of an unfortunate administration, lost one-third of its population. According to Chinese records, during the period from the third century BC to the present day, only 729 years have not suffered from natural catastrophes. All the others, at least 1400 of them, have been more or less affected by droughts, floods, or earthquakes (of which more anon, in the section on troglodyte dwellings). In twenty-three centuries China has suffered 1057 droughts and 1030 catastrophic floods.

Despite a more equable climate, Japan has not been free from disasters. Between 1690 and 1840 there were twenty-two famines, of which eleven were particularly severe and that of 1839 worst of all. The damage caused by volcanic eruptions and earthquakes, even including the Tokyo earthquake of 1923, has been slight compared with that due to floods and droughts.

THE VEXATIOUS ORGANISATION OF TRADITIONAL TRADE

Peasant income was reduced by the low prices at which agricultural products could be sold. The organisation of trade was such that the cost of transport, and expensive middlemen, greatly reduced the prices paid to the farmers. And the results were made worse by handling charges and the speculation of merchants. The author witnessed the following in Anhwei and in Kiangsu: wheat traders went into the countryside at the harvest time (May–June), spreading the rumour that the price of wheat was high. On hearing this, the peasants took their harvested wheat to the nearest market, whereupon the merchants banded together to quote a low price. What were the peasants to do? Return home with their heavy burden? This would have been an arduous task, and inept at that, for the moneylender to whom the peasant was indebted would have seen the wheat being transported, and the affair would not have escaped the notice of the landowner, to whom, in order to reduce the amount handed over, the peasant had given a false report of the amount harvested. Would it not be easier to conceal some paper money rather than sacks of wheat, if it was kept in the house? Finally, some local official, acting as an accomplice of the merchants, would threaten to requisition all the wheat in the market at a lower price than that quoted by the merchants. So the peasant sold to the merchant, who offered the higher price. The peasants were isolated in confrontation with the organised and disciplined guilds of merchants who fixed prices and forbade their members to buy dearer.

All too often the peasant, in order to pay his debts and taxes, had to sell at the time of harvest when the price was at its lowest; then for his own food and his supply of seed he had to repurchase later on, when the price was much higher. Chinese peasants would sell their rice at 10 Chinese dollars a picul (60 kg), at harvest time, and then buy rice in the spring at 28 dollars. Tonkinese farmers sold their harvest to wholesalers, who sold it back to them, several months later, at two-and-a-half times the price.

A large part of the value of the product so laboriously harvested by the peasant could be absorbed by middlemens' profits. A picul of tea bought for 1.5 dollars in Anhwei would be sold for 14 dollars in Shanghai market, after having passed through ten intermediary hands. The sale of a standing crop could also lower the price paid to the producer, and the very high cost of transport inevitably had the same effect.

EXCEPTIONAL EXPENSES

Peasant budgets could be seriously upset by expenses that were unforeseen, considerable and inevitable. There was no reserve of cash with which to face them. Moreover, it was quite unthinkable to refuse to pay for things which might seem absurd but which were demanded by social customs. A loan was the only way to meet such expenses.

The most frequent occasions were marriages and funerals. A son's marriage and a father's death, in most Far Eastern countries, cost about fifty of the normal monetary units. These 50 piastres, or yuen, or yen, represented about one-third of the annual income of a peasant family and an appreciable part of their inheritance. True, the peasant could seek assistance from his relatives and fellow citizens, as we shall see later on; but he would have to bear the major part of the cost himself. Often it would be necessary to mortgage some property in order to raise the cash. Chinese peasants, pious but impoverished, have sometimes sold themselves as slaves to obtain enough money for their father's funeral.

The pawning of a piece of land is only resorted to with great reluctance, for the peasants are deeply attached to the fields that they have inherited from their ancestors. The contracts of sale and repurchase are framed with this in mind; the land is sold below the normal price, but the seller reserves the right to repurchase at the same price within a certain time. The purchaser receives as interest the entire harvest of the land involved (though he may take on the seller as a sharecropper or tenant farmer). The purchaser, who acts as pawnbroker, takes no risk and has the chance of remaining as the owner of the land at a favourable price.

These exceptional expenses were conducive to usury. But it

was not always exceptional expenses that led in this direction, for quite often current expenses could involve moneylending. Farmers would find themselves at sowing time with no reserve of seed grain; so they had to borrow money to buy some. The rural areas of China benefited from these pawnbroking or money-lending services, which generally charged interest of 40 per cent per annum. In the villages a loan (in kind) of seed would be repaid six months later at 100 per cent (an interest rate of 200 per cent per annum); but by tradition this was accepted as normal.

Where did real usury begin? For small sums the interest rate could reach 150 per cent for six months, or 300 per cent per annum. Poverty and usury had led, in some parts of China, to a general peasant indebtedness that was a real social malady. For example, in one north Chinese village in 1932, 44 per cent of the families were in debt. Another village of twenty-five families owed a local moneylender a capital sum of 3000 Chinese dollars and an annual interest of 900 dollars, or an average of 36 dollars per family, though the annual income of each family was only 150 dollars. It was thus impossible for the peasants to extinguish their debts or even to pay off the accrued interest. They were obliged to sell their products to the moneylender at whatever price he chose to fix; in practice, the peasants of a village that had fallen so completely into debt gave to the moneylender all that they had to sell, but received no money in exchange, because the proceeds did not even suffice to pay the interest on the debt. The moneylender would grant the peasants a small new loan to ensure that they did not run away and continued to work for him. The complete absence of any agricultural banking system made it impossible to remedy these abuses.

The custom of usury was deeply ingrained. The female vege-table pedlars of the town of Hanoi borrowed each morning the sum of 2 French francs (in 1932) to buy vegetables that they sold from door to door. At the end of the day they paid back to the moneylender the sum of 2 francs 10 centimes, retaining whatever profit they had made from their sales. The money-lender had gained 5 per cent in one day — what incredible rate per annum? It is true that he was only concerned with such small business, and it occupied all his time.

The Japanese peasants, before 1940, had a higher standard of life than the Chinese. The annual expenditure (in money, and consumption of own produce) of a Japanese peasant family was 928 yen in 1926; half of this went on food, a lower percentage than was to be found elsewhere. This was a sign of the greater affluence in rural Nippon. Similarly, a Japanese family spent six times as much in a year on clothes as a Chinese family. Internal law and order, the well-developed transport system and rapid technical progress in all directions easily account for the Japanese superiority. However, the Japanese advantage was less than would appear from the crude figures, for social costs and taxation were much higher in Japan. Also, despite the Japanese advantage, the Nipponese countryfolk were reduced to desperate extremities, like selling their young daughters into prostitution. A rural exodus was already swelling the cities.

The Far Eastern peasants lived very inexpensively because they purchased as little as possible. They tended towards a closed family economy without quite attaining it. The economy was based on the family and not on the village, for the peasant did not find in the village the products that he did not produce himself. The village was a collection of family cells with little economic interrelation while each one of them had commercial relations with the world outside for the sale of agricultural produce and manufactured articles, and for divers purchases.

There were many differences between the countries in the 1930s. The Japanese countrysides were enclosed within a very dense commercial framework, and the Japanese peasants made relatively large purchases. The peasants of Cochinchina made almost none of the objects that they used. Elsewhere, peasant families lived almost exclusively for themselves, constrained by poverty to practise the most strictly closed economy.

CHAPTER 12

THE PEASANT FRAMEWORK: ANCIENT PRINCIPLES

In nature, all men are alike; by education they become completely different.

If a mere song gives celebrity in a country, then virtue no longer gives any.

Chinese proverbs

The traditional peasantries of the Far East existed in a solid framework comprising the family, the clan, the village and the state. A texture of local institutions (that might be regarded as the 'weft') and a hierarchy of political institutions belonging to the state (that could be looked on as the 'warp') created a vast and durable woven framework that made Far Eastern civilisation particularly effective, in controlling vast numbers of people spread over vast territories, for thousands of years. The dominant characteristic of the human geography of the Far East up to 1940 was the existence of densely packed peasantries scattered over wide spaces. This goes back to the dawn of written history, and it can not be explained without referring to the efficiency of the civilisation and its 'peopling' quality (see p. 25).

Because the institutions were more powerful than individuals, and the political framework depended on institutions rather than on the whims of a king, the peasants found in the traditional Chinese set-up some degree of protection against despotism; serfdom was abolished in China long before it disappeared from Europe. Chinese civilisation was imbued with moral principles that were applicable to both peasants and *literati*, and affirmed the fundamental equality of men.

THE IDEAL OF MODERATION

One had only to make the acquaintance of the peasants to be struck by their intelligence and cunning, their ability to avoid being imposed upon, and the strong critical spirit that lay concealed beneath a deferential manner. 'Large fish eat little fish, little fish eat shrimps, and the shrimps are obliged to eat muck'; so ran the Chinese dictum — but the shrimps retain their liberty and freedom of movement and are ready to change their circumstances with great agility. The peasants might be crushed by poverty, but they retained the deepseated conviction, derived from their civilisation, that it was not their inevitable lot to be poor and oppressed.

It is impossible to understand the mentality of the peasants without recognising that, although quite illiterate, they were imbued with the intellectual and moral principles of their civilisation. One of these was the ideal of moderation in all things (though of course this did not prevent some individuals from elbowing their way ahead of others and seeking to get rich). Said the philosopher Lao Tseu: 'He who is satisfied is always happy.' Many other sayings and proverbs confirm the same ideal: 'When good fortune comes along, don't spend it all at once'; 'Better to miss a bargain than to make an offer.' The same sentiments appear in the words painted on the red paper strips that are affixed to doorposts at the New Year: 'An untroubled spirit brings good fortune; patience is the best family heritage', and the same moderation should guide the steps of the elite: 'In a badly-governed state the Wise Man keeps himself out of harm's way by being silent.'

The Confucian ideals of the happy medium, of solving disagreements by conciliation and of diffidence towards anything absolute were reinforced by the Taoist ideals of non-resistance and self-effacement: 'Do not aspire to be the first person in the universe', said Lao Tseu. All this is commonly revealed in the extreme concern for 'face-saving', which is an essential part of the machinery of Chinese social relations. Casual travellers and serious students alike are agreed on the importance of 'face' in Chinese social life. In a conflict of interests, as in a dispute, it is unbecoming to pour scorn on the guilty (or the weaker) party; he should be left with his battle-honours. This desire for face-saving, pushed to its ultimate limit, could take all the spice out of sporting contests — imagine a football match with each side preoccupied with saving the face of its adversary!

The fewer the demands one makes on one's fellowmen, the less the chance of being deceived: 'Choose the least demanding way to happiness' said a sage in the late Ming period (seventeenth century). One of the ways to attain such happiness was communion with nature, through the calm enjoyment of natural beauty: 'If you do not shelter from the raindrops, you will find them very beautiful', said another seventeenth-century writer.

THE IDEAL OF DISCIPLINE

It has often been remarked that the Chinese are undisciplined; they walk across lawns in complete disregard of the prohibitory notices, they cut firewood from young trees on the edge of new forest plantations, and so on. But one should not give too much weight to such examples; lawns and reafforestation do not form part of the traditional world of the peasant, and their education has not taught them to respect such things. The peasants have a strong sense of discipline, but, as we noted above, this discipline must come willingly and through conciliation. 'Don't push your fellowmen against the wall', says a Chinese proverb.

> States, dogmas and laws can do nothing to promote discipline. Discipline is conceived as a state of peace that abstract reasoning cannot impose. What is necessary to attain this peaceful state is a liking for conciliation that requires an acute sense of actual expediency and spontaneous fellowship. . . . The idea of discipline contains within itself . . . the feeling that to know and to understand one another is to be at peace with oneself and with the outside world. The whole wisdom of the Chinese philosophy is contained in this notion.[1]

[1] M. Granet, *La Pensée chinoise*, 1934.

RELIGIOUS THOUGHT

The Chinese had the same attitude towards religion.

> One might characterise the spirit of Chinese customs by the
> formula: neither God nor law. It has often been said that the
> Chinese had no religion. . . . The truth is that in China
> religion, like the law, is not a separate social function. . . . A
> feeling for the sacred plays a great part in Chinese life, but the
> objects of veneration are not gods. . . . The Almighty has a
> literacy existence only. . . . Confucians and Taoists alike give
> no consideration to an omnipotent deity. For them, the only
> sacred beings are the Taoist Saints and the Confucian Wise
> Men. . . . They have no conception of gods that are strangers
> to mankind, having an essence of their own. . . . They do not
> think about a god or gods. . . . There is no organised clergy, so
> gods have no point of contact with mankind. . . . The Chinese
> attitude towards the past (if they do not just eliminate it from
> their thoughts) is one of quiet familiarity. . . . No Chinese
> philosopher has ever attempted to found a way of life based
> on divine sanctions. . . . Chinese wisdom is completely in-
> dependent and completely human.[1]

There is no fear of what lies beyond this life; when asked to
speak about death Confucius replied, 'I do not understand life, so
how can I comprehend death?'

All this contrasts markedly with the rigidity imposed by the
Chinese communists in order to overcome the non-communists.
Not only are the dissidents overcome, but they are made to lose
face by being obliged to declare that they are mistaken and that
they have deceived their fellow-citizens. These public humilia-
tions (which, however, have not replaced penal sanctions such as
prison or the death penalty), are quite contrary to the principle
of respect for 'face'. Does this represent a mental revolution, or is
it the expression of other undercurrents of Chinese thought, such
as the irresistible efficiency (which it would be criminal to
oppose) of a power that has a mandate from Heaven, or the notion
that repression is justified if it is in the cause of a just principle like

[1] *Ibid.*

respect for the right way, respect for virtue and the command from above?

How have the essential elements of traditional Chinese thought been so brutally dispersed, leaving the field clear for a communist absolutism that admits neither the traditional modes of thought (though this is by no means certain) nor family organisation, nor respect for the opinions of others, nor moderation, nor political indifference? It is possible that the vast majority of the Chinese people really believe that Heavenly power left the Kuomintang and passed to the communist party. The state of discredit and debility into which the Kuomintang had sunk are contrasted with the solidity, the unbroken continuity and the relative success of the communists. The next half-century will decide whether the present communist regime is simply an episode in a long history that extends over nearly 5000 years, or whether it is an irreversible trend.

It is worth remembering that the communist conviction that for mankind all things are possible (a conviction, however, that by neglecting the time factor has led to serious errors) is not completely incompatible with an essential tenet of the ancient Chinese religion. The ancient Chinese were obsessed by the fear that the seasons would cease to follow one another in normal succession, and that the oceans and continents, mountains and plains, might change their respective situations. They combated this obsession by trying to influence and placate the supernatural powers through rites that would ensure the regular sequence of seasons. Thus traditional Chinese opinion was that human action influenced the seasons and the distribution of land and sea, mountain and plain; and hence the belief in the ultimate power of human intervention. The Son of Heaven was master of the earth and the waters, of time and space.

CHAPTER 13

THE PEASANT FAMILY

When you buy a pig, you examine the sow that bore it;
When you take a wife, you discover her ancestry.
When I am hungry, I like to eat the fruit of the cucumber tree and the sycamore
But if I see my mother-in-law I can't stomach them.
Chinese pirates are less cruel than a husband's sisters.

Popular Vietnamese songs

Encourage filial piety, fraternal love, and agriculture: these are clichés for mandarin gatherings.

Unofficial history of the 'literati' (18th-century Chinese novel)

FAMILY LINKS

The rural societies of the Far East were in the first place collections of families. One of the most deeprooted ideas in Chinese social and political philosophy was that if each family lived in a disciplined fashion and respected the traditions, the state by this very fact would be well governed and prosperous. 'The princes of old, in order to make their natural virtues shine in the hearts of men, endeavoured above all to ensure good government for their respective principalities. And in order to do this, they began by maintaining good order in their own families.' Good family relationships set an example; disorder within the family was a matter for the state, which could and should intervene to restore domestic harmony.

The family was an autonomous unit, imposing on its members an authority quite unknown in the Western world, since the state delegated responsibility to it. On the other hand, the state could be induced to intervene to punish faults that we should regard as quite outside the sphere of politics — such as disrespect of parents by children. 'A family whose members are polite and considerate spreads politeness and consideration amongst its fellow-citizens. Loose-living and perversity of a single member stirs up strife and disorder amongst the whole people.' 'Courtesy will be richly rewarded.' 'Charm is humanity.' Of the 120 volumes of the *General Chronicles of the Province of Anhwei* (1878 edition) four are devoted to the enumeration of dutiful sons, four to upright citizens and thirty to chaste widows.

The family was a very strong organisation; it was at one and the same time a miniature state, with the father as monarch, a farm, in which both labour and rewards were shared among the members, and a church, with the head of the family as the chief priest. The authority of the family head was thus very powerful in all directions; it extended even to condemning to death a son who by his disrespect and disobedience had dishonoured the family name.

Within this general pattern, how many individuals constituted a family? A family ought to comprise all the descendants of a common paternal ancestor. But in reality a large number of the individuals who could regard themselves as having a common paternal ancestor could not live together as a family; they would form a clan, and this kind of organisation was much more solid and influential in southern China than in the north. Usually, an autonomous family would comprise five or six persons grouped around the paternal head of the family — father, mother, children and perhaps a grandparent. There were many larger families since one or more married sons might live under the paternal roof, but this demanded a certain degree of wealth. The size of a Chinese family living together depended, indeed, on the family fortune; poor families were reduced in size by death and migration. If a small autonomous family had only a younger son as its head there was no ancestral altar, and the family cult was sustained in the house of the eldest brother.

Without disappearing, the family ties weakened in the next

generation; the eldest son of a younger son would venerate his father by erecting an ancestral altar and would himself become the head of a quasi-autonomous family. The religious ties with the elder branch of the family would not be broken, but would be stretched.

The descendants of a common ancestor would have a collective place of worship, where they would gather on fixed dates. They recognised among themselves a genuine kinship, which had expression in the prohibition of marriage between members of the group. The family name was really no indication of these exogamous groups, for patronymics were few in number – no more than a hundred, perhaps, in the whole of China or Vietnam. If marriage had been forbidden in Vietnam, for example, between men and women bearing the name Nguyen, few marriages would have been possible, for 40 per cent of all the Vietnamians in Tonkin were so called.

Kinship linkages were recorded in genealogical trees kept by the various small families belonging to a larger family group; for example, five generations from a common ancestor formed a family tree, smaller than a clan. Such a group of small families had a certain cohesion and a degree of solidarity. The members of this 'extended family' felt that they belonged to an honourable society of living and dead, and it was their duty not to lessen the standing of the group. They took care that no member of the family group committed any dishonourable act. If however, such a contingency did arise, the family would endeavour to conceal the misdemeanour and avert an ignominious punishment. Family solidarity was also expressed in the shared responsibility of the members. Thus if one member should commit some rebellious act all his relatives would be punished, for the entire family was considered to have been corrupted.

The most dreadful crime of parricide, the murder of a parent, would be followed by punishment not merely of the family but of the entire village; the chief mandarin of the district in which the crime was committed would be severely reprimanded for not having set a sufficiently virtuous example to his people. The principle of collective responsibility was moreover a condition of family solidarity, for in saving one of their relatives the members were protecting themselves.

FILIAL PIETY

The head of a family had in theory an almost absolute authority; he controlled the property and could punish the members of the family, eject them, sell them or even put them to death. The authority of the family head did not bow to any dignity acquired by one of the members; if a high-ranking functionary returned to his native village, he gave way to his elders who might be just simple peasants.

In practice the authority of a father was rather more limited. True, the children had nothing of their own; their wages went to their father (who undertook, however, to be responsible for any debts that the children might contract). In fact the father would administer the property in conjunction with his adult sons, and their signatures would be appended to any documents relating to the patrimony. Daily life put many restrictions on the authority of a family head, and a peasant could not become a domestic tyrant.

Filial devotion gave great prestige to the head of the family. Custom required that a son should show respect for, and obedience to, his parents. Chinese texts are full of principles and examples of filial piety. The realities may not quite have matched the principles, but filial devotion was certainly one of the most marked characteristics of Far Eastern society. Some examples may be cited. There was a young boy, eight years of age, whose parents were too poor to buy a mosquito net; he went to bed before his parents, and in the enclosed bedroom, without putting on the fan, exposed himself voluntarily to the bites of the mosquitoes, which were thus satiated by the time the parents retired. It is unfortunate that the son should die before his father, but when bereavements are a normal occurrence they are not regarded as catastrophes. Nevertheless, in Tonkin, when a young man dies before his father, it is regarded as a desertion, greeted by a reproving silence and a sense of humiliation. The funeral rites are therefore reduced to a minimum. An only son who found himself gravely ill would fervently wish that his father would die before him, so that he would have time to render the appropriate funeral honours. When a son died prematurely his body would be given a sham corporal chastisement; the corpse would be dressed in full mourning before being placed in the coffin; thus he would have fulfilled his filial duties by wearing the mourning prepared for his father's death.

'A son should follow the wishes of his father whilst the latter is alive, and his example, when he is dead. If, for three years, after the death of his father, he imitates his conduct in all ways, he may be said to practise filial piety.' 'If your parents are at fault, warn them with great gentleness. If they do not take your advice, redouble your respectful remonstrances. If they maltreat you, bear no resentment.' 'During the life of your parents, do not go too far away.' 'You must often recall the age of your parents, so that you may rejoice in their longevity and fear lest they should die.' 'A son should not dishonour his parents by mutilating the body that they gave him, but should return it whole to the earth.' 'Three things are contrary to filial piety. The first is to encourage parents to do wrong, by blandishments and culpable complacency; the second is to be unwilling to get a well-paid job that would help to relieve their poverty; the third is to have neither wife nor children and so to cut off the parents from ancestral devotions. Of the three faults, the greatest is to remain without descendants.' Filial piety can be expressed in the most delicate fashion: 'one should respect one's parents; see how the lamb and the kid go down on their knees when their mother suckles them'; it is true that this is a much-used cliché in Chinese literature.

The general sentiment of filial devotion had as a natural consequence a respect for old age that was one of the most honourable characteristics of Far Eastern civilisation. Old people were venerated in their capacity as heads of families, and because their longevity was a sign of the benevolence of the supernatural powers and an indication of good augury for the village that had the honour of sheltering them. In order to retain favours of this kind old people were much coddled, and even given a special diet. Some districts in the Red River delta gave their old folk warm clothing that their families could not afford to buy.

ANCESTOR WORSHIP

The dead were devoutly worshipped. They were very carefully

buried because it was believed that the body must be returned intact to the earth. The tombs were small earth mounds, usually located on the poor soils of the hillsides; sometimes they would be dug in one of the family fields, where the mound marking their position would be slowly eroded by ploughing.

Ancestor worship was performed before an altar erected within the dwelling-house. In China, as in Vietnam, the altar is more or less richly ornamented; it usually comprises one or more tables that carry the reliquary containing the memorial tablets of five generations of ancestors; tablets of earlier generations are placed in a family temple, where they receive only a form of worship common to all family ancestors. In Japan, among the Shintoist families, the altar is a small model of a Shinto temple, constructed, like the actual temple, without any nails (since the Shinto temples preserve the ancient Japanese techniques of house-building), and placed on the 'shelf of the gods' that was attached to one of the partition walls. This reliquary contains the white wooden tablets on which are inscribed the names of the ancestors. If the family honours its ancestors in the Buddhist fashion, the altar is a reliquary resting on a shelf above an alcove; the tablets are lacquered and bear inscriptions in letters of gold.

The principal seasons for ancestor worship are the New Year, death anniversaries, and various dates such as the twenty-third day of the second moon, with offerings of peach-flowers in spring and chrysanthemums in the autumn. Several times a month, the ancestors are honoured with sticks of incense and offerings of prepared food and drink. In Japan, women and old people may perform daily ancestor worship, with prayers and a libation of tea.

In the traditional peasant beliefs, the dead are still part of the family; their souls, or their transformed bodies, are not far away. To remain in a state of contentedness they must have the sight and the aroma of prepared food; they must not be neglected, and they wish to be kept informed of family happenings such as marriages and births; they require both respect and material gifts.

Thus placated, the dead help and protect the living. If neglected, the ancestry become unhappy and vindictive; they provoke innumerable untoward happenings and bring nightmares to the undutiful son, who is quickly made to toe the line by his own fright and by pressure from scandalised and terrified neighbours — for this persecution of errant souls can extend to persons quite unrelated to the real victims. It is thus generally desirable that everyone should be faithful in the worship of his ancestors. As a further precaution, some villages maintained one or more small chapels where sacrifices were regularly made to the unburied dead and to those whose worship had been abandoned. Persons dying without leaving an heir who could worship them bequeathed to the village a field the rent from which would pay for decent regular worship. Any peasant who had acquired some degree of wealth would not fail to endow his lineage with a small ancestral temple and some inalienable land that would provide money for worship.

The respect for ancestors could lead to some peculiar 'kidnappings'. Malefactors, having violated a tomb and stolen the skull of the father of a wealthy personage, would announce that the remains would be restored on payment of a ransom. The son is fearful for the repose of his father's soul and for his own peace of mind, because the disturbed soul would torment him. So what to do? Inform the authorities (who were disposed to deal very severely with such cases)? But if the thieves destroyed the father's remains, no good would come from their punishment. It would be better to pay the ransom, and hope that the thieves would not say a little later on that the restored skull was not the authentic one, and demand another ransom. Much ado about a single skull. The Far Eastern respect for ancestral tombs gave the authorities a sanction against rebels; in difficult cases a bandit would be threatened with the destruction of the tombs of his ancestors.

GUARDIAN SPIRITS AND DEVILS

Ancestor worship was not the only aspect of the religious life of the Far Eastern peasants. Among the Chinese peasants there remained distinct traces of animism that official philosophic doctrine had not succeeded in eradicating. It is true that many peasants, devoid of mystical emotion, considered that the worship of domestic gods was useless, but it was inoffensive, unembarrassing, and the women liked it — a veritable pascalian sentiment. There was little sentiment in all this, but simply the performance of rites that varied the daily monotony.

The domestic divinities were numerous; spirits lurked in every corner of the house, and there were spirits of the harvest, of various illnesses, and a hundred other animist deifications. Most important was the spirit of the hearth, honoured in the kitchen; he ascended to Heaven at the end of the year, at which time his effigy was burnt, after his lips had been smeared with sugar so that he could carry with him only sweet recollections of the people of the house. Outside the habitual rites, many exceptional occasions required ceremonies designed to beguile or restrain the spirits, who were regarded by the peasants as timorous, vain and easy to deceive. When as epidemic of cholera occurred during the summer, resulting from the consumption of polluted water and water-melons, the New Year festival was celebrated (which actually occurs in winter); the usual inscriptions in black letters on red paper were fixed to the doors, and thus deceived, the cholera devil thought that he had mistaken the date (because cholera epidemics are always in the summer) and that he had better put back the epidemic to a later time.

Outside the house, the Chinese peasants paid homage to the agricultural spirits; on New Year's Day, they would go to the various village temples to burn incense candles to the deities. But they would not return to the temples again before the following year. Women were the gods' most faithful clients; they would go regularly to the Buddhist pagoda, there to meet with friends out of sight of their husbands.

The cults of domestic worship were no less numerous in Japan; within the house homage would be paid to the god of the well, the goddesses of rice and of the silkworm, the gods of the winds, the cooking pot, the stewpan, the gods of fire, wood and metal, and the gods of the latrines who taught the people how to fertilise their fields.

The Japanese peasants, at least up to the beginning of the twentieth century, remained faithful to a Shintoist religion that was more than a merely local affair. In the province of Izumo, a devout Shintoist would rise early, wash his face and his mouth, and then turn towards the sun, clap his hands, bow his head and say 'greetings to thee this day, Lord of all things', an invocation that was also used in homage to Tenno, the Emperor, a direct descendant of the Sun. He then prostrated himself in the direction of the imperial palace. Afterwards he would pray before the ancestral altar; on his knees, he would call upon the deities of Izumo, those of the major provincial temples, the spirit of the village, thanking his ancestors for the home that they had founded.

The Shinto religion, being naturist in character, led to the contemplation and love of nature. The Japanese deeply enjoyed their countryside. Here is an anecdote that is symptomatic of this attitude: crossing Paris one day, a Japanese saw the first snowfall of winter; he immediately hurried to the Bois de Boulogne to admire the trees that bore snow on their every branch and twig; the paths were deserted, and then he spied another walker — who was also from Nippon! In what other country, even in the Far East, would the crowds flock to admire famous landscapes, and in contemplating them, commune with the most subtle depths of their culture. Can peasants be found anywhere but in Japan, who will travel miles in the small hours in order to witness the sudden opening of a lotus flower in the first rays of sunlight, or stop to admire the cherry blossom, or the vivid autumn colours of the maples, the reflection of the moon in a lake, and to derive from these sights a pleasure equal to that of listening to a charming singer on the radio or playing cards in an inn. In ancient China, the *literati* experienced these things — as the charming memoirs of Chen Fou clearly show; but the Chinese peasants knew nothing of this.

Pilgrimages, for religious as well as aesthetic reasons, played a great part in the life of rural Japan, where most peasants had been to one or other of the country's holy places. In China, such things were less important; however, crowds of the faithful did move towards particularly celebrated sites like the mountain O Mei (in Szechwan), the island of Pou To (in the Chusan archipelago at the mouth of the Ning Po River), the mountains Ou Tai (in Shansi), and Tai Chan (in Shantung). In northern Vietnam the Buddhist shrine of Huong Tich attracted large numbers.

The pilgrims would see beautiful landscapes, for the pagodas and temples were generally tastefully sited (Fig. 13.1); they

Fig. 13.1 A pilgrimage centre. The temple of Hong Chan, west of Chang Cha, in Honan province; perched on a hilltop, like O Meichan in Szechwan, or Tai Chan in Shantung

would sleep in the attractive timberframe buildings set aside for visitors, and would listen to the sacristans' stories of the lives of the wise men and saints. Besides these great pilgrimage centres, many local sites would attract the faithful of the neighbourhood on certain dates; such 'pilgrims' would come simply as a diversion from the normal routine, or to seek a cure for certain ailments, notably sterility and mental illness.

CHILDREN

Births were numerous, partly because of a complete lack of control measures, and partly through the desire of every father to have a male heir to ensure ancestor worship. Chinese Buddhism led in the same direction; those who believed in successive reincarnations — and the peasants were all more or less imbued with this doctrine — thought that to have no children was a punishment inflicted for sins committed in a previous existence. For a man this was humiliating, and he would develop an inferiority complex through not being surrounded by children, and especially by sons. For a woman, to fail to give birth to a son was a cause of sadness and tribulation, leading to the husband's bad temper and the chaffing of the neighbours. She might have to permit a concubine in the house, and might actually be repudiated. However, an adoption could enable the head of the family to ensure the continuity of ancestor worship.

The boy population of China was greater than that of girls; a sample study made in 1935 showed 123 boys for every 100 girls, under the age of ten. This abnormal situation resulted from the 'suppression' of some girl babies and a more general neglect of girls, who were generally considered to be a liability because they did not bring any compensation to the father on their marriage; once married they were lost to their original family and so could not contribute to the support of their father in his old age; sons were the best security against old age.

The child would be suckled by the mother so long as she was under no obligation to wean it. In the case of a boy he would be presented to the ancestors at the age of one month; for a girl the mother would burn a stick of incense in the nearest pagoda or Shinto temple. At first the child would be given a very vulgar name, so that the evil demons would not bother to touch such a reprehensible object. A girl might be called 'little sow', a boy, in Korea, 'villainous cutthroat', or 'dog-turd'.

Infantile diseases caused enormous ravages in China; many fatalities were caused by wiping children's eyes with a shirt hem or a dirty rag; at a very early age babies ate a little of everything — they were often given rice that their mother had already chewed, a good method of predigestion, perhaps, but not to be recommended. When a child had convulsions, the mother would hold it to her body in a very tight embrace, so as to draw off some of the 'bad fluid'; certainly this helped to quiet the child.

Parents treated their children with affection and kindness; children in the country had an especially happy time, provided they were not hungry. Parents were also very proud of their offspring. 'No one sees any faults in his children nor any beauty in his harvest', said a rather malicious Chinese proverb.

The achievements and gestures of the small child were of great interest to the parents, who would soon want to know what he would grow up to be. At the age of one year the child would be placed on a mat strewn with symbolic objects such as a warrior's bow, a merchant's abacus, a writer's pencil, and a flower (the sign of a frivolous and dissolute character); by clutching at one of these the infant would give some indication of his preference. Of course, no significance was placed on the experiment if the infant seized either the bow or the flower (the bearing of arms was not a popular occupation in China). 'High quality iron doesn't make nails and brave men don't make soldiers.'

In her spare moments — of which she had all too few — a mother would recount to her children the story of the Flying Heads who used their ears as wings, the tale of the sparrow that turned itself into a frog, of the rat that changed into a quail, and the story of the old man in the moon whose task it was to join by an invisible silk thread a boy and a girl who were destined for each other; or the exploits of the first emperor, who shot down with arrows six or seven moons that once shone in the sky, and stories of foxes that got changed into women.

Children played many games; shuttlecock was the most widespread, and they made kites and paddled in the ponds. Parents allowed them a great deal of liberty; their indulgence and patience were food for thought for a Westerner. The boisterousness of youth left no traces; uncontrollable children became docile adults and dutiful sons; a small child was neither slapped nor thwarted, but social pressure was so great that in growing up the children submitted to their parents without any opposition.

At six or seven years of age, Chinese children could go to school; but over much of China, despite the respect with which learning was surrounded, many children never went to school because the nearest one was too far away, and because education, without being expensive, was not entirely free.

The traditional small school has persisted for a very long time in China. Run by a literate person who had not managed to get into the mandarin clique, it taught the children Chinese characters. Under the master's stick, which he did not hesitate to use even though the children were not beaten at home, the scholars learned the characters in a series of monotonous exercises. The study of these characters inculcated in the children the fundamental ideas of Chinese civilisation; the first phrase learnt in school was 'By his origin and nature man is a saint', for one of the essential themes in Chinese philosophy is the inherent goodness of man. The first poem learnt in school taught the child the ideals of simple communion with nature and quiet contentment put forward by the Chinese wise men: 'Carried by the warm breeze, the fleecy clouds float in the sky at daybreak; entranced by the flowery banks, I wander ever further; people will say, the old man is looking for adventure, when in fact my soul is sailing on towards good fortune.'

Most of the pupils at such schools soon forgot the little that they had learnt. They had not mastered enough characters to be able to read a quite easy text. To read or write a letter they had to seek the schoolmaster's assistance. The Japanese, in contrast, had been able to organise a modern form of education that all children could readily follow.

THE TREATMENT OF GIRLS

At first the small girl leads the same life as her brother; but, until quite recently, at about the age of eight the girl would suffer a prolonged martyrdom, the mutilation of the feet. By massage and tightening bandages, the toes and the whole external part of the metatarsal area were folded under the foot; by reason of the exaggerated concavity of the soles, the body weight rested on the big toe and the tip of the heel. After many years the mutilated foot became the 'golden water-lily' dear to the hearts of Chinese poets and a source of aesthetic and sensual emotion to men. The mutilation of feet was never practised outside China, and it is no longer the custom in China today. It had one advantage in that it prevented women from doing heavy work of the kind that was customary among the women of Vietnam and Japan. It was simply a trait of the civilisation, serving no useful purpose whatsoever.

In Far Eastern society women played an inferior role. Theoretically at least they should always obey a man, whether it be

father, husband, or son. As a matter of principle, female nature
was inferior to masculine (and most things were classed as either
masculine or feminine), and was uncertain, suspect and meet to
be subordinated. The rigid separation of the sexes, although not
absolute in the country districts, was not practised to safeguard
the purity of the females but to protect the males from a degrading influence. Custom and the law removed from the female
all initiative and all will; even ancestor worship gave but an acces-
sory role to women and scarcely regarded them as persons.

Although not well received at birth by parents who would
have to feed her until her marriage and then lose her, the small
girl was raised with affection; she learnt at her mother's side the
domestic chores and work in the fields. But the parents would be
anxious to get her married off, and quite soon would begin to
contrive an intrigue that would rid them of an unproductive
mouth and lead to a few presents for themselves (for the fiancé's
gifts were not all returned to the young couple). In Tonkin the
girl's parents would gently hint to the fiancé's parents that 'a pig
is fattened to produce lard, and children are reared in the
expectation of some benefit'.

For a woman, marriage was a particularly important event. She
was leaving the family, in which she had never been ill-treated,
and entering a new family of which she knew nothing. Often,
indeed, the young girl had never even seen her future husband
before the day of the ceremony. The marriage would be preceded
by a formal betrothal agreement written on red paper (the colour
signifying joy); the family of the intended husband would clinch
the deal with gifts. Usually these betrothals were decided on
when the couple were still in childhood, and infants could even
be affianced before their birth. The interested parties were thus
never consulted; marriage was a family affair, not one of personal
preference.

It could thus happen that the family of the affianced boy and
that of the intended bride had never even met before the
wedding-day. The union would have been organised not by direct
conversation between the respective parents but through an intermediary. A Chinese family would be well acquainted only with
its kinsfolk, among whom it was almost impossible to find a
young man and a young woman who could fulfil the necessary

requirements. Marriage custom was very strict; relatives with a common paternal ancestor, however far back, could not marry; prohibitions on the maternal ancestor side were less severe. It was thus difficult to find a possible partner in a village peopled by cousins with a common paternal ancestor. Hence the recourse to intermediaries — women of wide experience, who knew all the families in a district (canton), their wealth and the qualities and defects of all the marriageable children. Solicited by the fathers of boys and of girls in need of partners, the intermediary would busy herself trying to make matches by the giving of presents. Her intervention was of great value to the Chinese in avoiding direct discussions and perhaps ill-advised promises that might lead to loss of face. When all the arrangements had been made by the intermediary, the families would finally meet — without the young couple. In Korea and Vietnam the intermediaries were men, not women.

Astrological indications would determine the date of the wedding; for every human being was considered to have been placed, by the year, month and day of his birth, under a series of astrological and terrestrial influences; if by any chance the horoscopes of the bride and bridegroom were found to be in conflict, the betrothal would be broken off.

In China — and it was much the same in the other Far Eastern countries — when the wedding day arrived, the young man would go to the house of his fiancée, and she would be delivered to him, draped in a red veil, by her parents; he would see her into a red-painted rickshaw and hurry on in advance so as to be able to greet her arrival at his parent's house. Even among the peasants all these things were done with great pomp, amidst a great crowd of relatives and friends, and to the accompaniment of salvoes of shots that would keep off the evil spirits. Every effort would be made to build up portents of good fortune; the bride, on stepping from the carriage, had to jump over a saddle (the word *ngan* means both saddle and peace); she would receive a gift of jujubes and chestnuts (the words for jujube and chestnut form the phrase *tsao li tseu* which means 'have a son soon'). In the bridegroom's house, the major ceremonies were the adoration of Heaven and Earth and the ritual of the cups: the espoused couple would receive two goblets tied together with a red thread, would half-drain them, then exchange cups to finish the remainder. The marriage was thus concluded, without either a priest or a civil officer. The young wife would then lift her red veil and see her husband for the first time. She would greet her parents-in-law, and would then have to submit to a very severe test. In front of all the assembled relatives, friends, neighbours and indeed the whole village, she must listen to all kinds of most uncomplimentary remarks about herself, while remaining impassive, with not a reply, not a laugh nor a tear. A firm countenance would give her a reputation as a capable woman.

On the following day the young wife would bow to the ancestral tablets and the spirit of the household. If the family had means, there would be a banquet lasting a day or two, with the men separated from the women. Finally the husband would go to the wife's former home and salute the ancestral tablets of her family.[1] Among the poorer folk, not all the rites would be followed. Sometimes they would buy a small girl who had been brought up with the children of the house to become the son's wife. Marriage with a widow was less expensive because it could be arranged with no ceremonies and no presents. In Korea, it could be achieved simply by the violation of the woman (usually with consent) by the intended husband.

By her marriage, a woman changed her family and her ancestral line; her husband's ancestors became her own. She would return but rarely to her birthplace, for such visits would encounter the hostility of her brothers' wives. However, the new family would hardly make her welcome; the wives of her husband's brothers would give her the cold shoulder, her mother-in-law would tyrannise and browbeat her, without her husband daring to offer any opposition to his mother. Of course these difficulties were always greater in large wealthy families, where the patriarch continued to be surrounded by all his sons; they would not arise in small families.

The young wife must 'make soup to her mother-in-law's taste, prepare her bed and bring her the chamber-pot'. The mother-in-law had the right to beat her — a right that was often abused. It

---

[1] In Vietnam the husband's family had to pay a marriage tax to the wife's village. In effect this was a civil registration of the marriage.

was not uncommon to find daughters-in-law killed by maltreatment, though the fear of reprisals taken by the family of the young wife placed some limit on the cruelty. If the family of the dead girl got to know the real cause of her death, they would endeavour to exploit the situation by claiming enormous damages and seeking to gain face at the expense of the culpable family. Such things were rare but not unknown. A young wife had no redress for maltreatment and was not entitled to flee. At length the daughter-in-law might gain the upper hand, and taking advantage of the decrepitude of the old lady, would let her perish from frustrated rage and lack of attention.

A husband would treat his wife with some care, although he possessed all the rights and the wife had no legal protection. He had the right to beat her, and if she committed adultery he could kill her without being prosecuted. Feminine adultery was in fact very rare, because of the severity of the law, because of village gossip and the extreme curiosity that all villagers showed in the private lives of their neighbours, and because of the many pre-occupations of the womenfolk. A husband could easily repudiate his wife: 'A woman is like a cloak; if it ceases to serve you, or looks worn-out, you can change it.'

The lot of the young wife improved as soon as she bore a son; henceforth she was a person of some importance in the family. But if she produced no sons, she must put up with the presence of a concubine, whose children were regarded as hers and called her mother, the real mother being known as aunt. In better-off families, indeed, it might well happen that the wife would choose a concubine for her husband.

We must not jump to the conclusion that life in China for the female peasant was necessarily unhappy. In most cases, her life was quite stable; she knew that she stood in no fear of repudiation; she usually ruled the family and her husband accepted her advice: 'combating the women needs extreme prudence'. But it nevertheless often happened that in order to impose her will, she had to have recourse to violent imprecations.

Female peasants had many jobs to do. On their shoulders fell the task of keeping the house clean (an absorbing occupation in Japan but accomplished more quickly in China and Vietnam), washing the meagre stock of linen, and cooking (which was much more time-taking if the maintenance of the fire proved difficult). She did less weaving than in former times, but she spun sufficient yarn for mending clothes. She cut out and stitched garments for the whole family, and kept them in good repair. In China she also made slippers, and padded garments to keep out the cold; in the spring she would unstitch these in order to get rid of the vermin which would otherwise be impossible to remove — and then of course they would have to be sewn up again. She would also work in the farmyard, which would not be far away, and might play some part in agricultural work. In Japan and in Tonkin she would perform the hardest tasks, such as the planting out of rice (a task allotted to the men in China), as well as dressing the soil with manure and weeding. In Tonkin women were also petty traders, dealing prudently with small businesses.

DAILY LIFE

Family life did not always accord with the degree of family feeling, for the house was often too small for the number of inhabitants, and lacked calm and privacy. It was a communal life, but without much intimacy; too often the relations between members of the family were strained and unnatural.

Furious quarrels would sometimes break out, in which mothers-in-law, daughters and daughters-in-law all joined. The word for 'dispute' in Chinese is written as two successive characters meaning 'woman'. Chinese and Vietnamian women possessed a great capacity for giving their cries a dramatic tone; neighbours would listen delightedly to the curses, while the head of the family, powerless to calm the storm, kept quiet or cleared out. Chinese women would sometimes climb on to the roof of the house in order to get a larger audience. This appeal to public opinion might achieve some success if the husband sensed that the general sentiment was not in his favour. Visitors to the villages frequently witnessed such scenes, which contributed a little variety to an otherwise monotonous existence. The drama usually left no traces other than exhausted vocal cords.

The Chinese honoured a certain Wise Man who had suc-ceeded in maintaining a serene existence in a house where nine generations of a family lived together. Astonished at this success, the Son of Heaven wished to know the secret of the harmony; the Wise Man then wrote several times the character meaning 'patience'. The image of this Wise Man, placed in the kitchen, was supposed to promote concord and goodwill in the family. It must be admitted that the environment in which the Wise Man lived must have been peculiarly soothing, for the legend adds that he kept a hundred dogs, so well-behaved that they waited for late-comers before eating their food!

Life in Japanese villages ran rather more smoothly. There was an atmosphere of courtesy that charmed all who experienced it. Thus Lafcadio Hearn: 'I lived in some parts where no thefts had been known to occur for hundreds of years, where the prisons recently constructed by the Meiji were empty and unused, and where the people never bothered to close their doors by night or by day.' A discipline imposed by long tradition had inculcated in the Japanese the idea that violent expression of sentiments was vulgar and degrading. Even the poorest peasant was convinced that sorrow and anger should not be manifested in public. If the most illiterate of peasants allowed himself to weep, his first words on regaining his composure would be 'pardon my selfish-ness and impoliteness'. Such manners were quite unknown in Chinese villages, and very far indeed from the coarse invective of the Chinese wife calling to her 'neighbours east and west'.

The monotony of daily life was not interrupted by a weekly 'Sunday'; such a regular pause was unknown in the Far East. But feast days did provide a useful distraction for the peasantry. The most important and most widely recognised was New Year's Day, in February, when the entire Far East gave itself over to celebra-tions (cf., p. 85). There were also seasonal feasts, in spring, summer, autumn and winter. In Japan the spring and autumn feasts were general ones for the entire village, whereas the summer and winter ones were more of a family nature, involving ancestor worship. And a peasant had to be really poor if he could not offer a small present to his children on the occasion of their own feasts, 3 March for little Japanese girls and 5 May for boys. Other feasts took place on family occasions such as the anniver-sary of the father's death, marriages or funerals. The expensive feasts given on such occasions often brought economic ruin to families (cf., p. 142), even though the participants offered some contribution, this never covered the cost since the family giving the feast was intent on entertaining as lavishly as possible. Such revelry was a source of great joy to the peasants; they ate far too much, got drunk on rice wine, and talked themselves out of breath.

CHAPTER 14

PEASANT HOUSES

The mountains of Szechwan were denuded in order
to build the palace of A-p'ang.

Chinese saying (3rd century BC)

THE HOUSE: EPITOME OF A CIVILISATION

Peasant houses in the Far East are not just a simple reflection, adapted to a certain physical environment, of the human need for shelter. As elsewhere, they are an amalgam of the facts of civilisation, in their techniques of construction, their architectural ideals, and their adaptation to social needs as conceived in the Far East. The house types that we shall describe show poor adaptation to climate, and a not very rational use of natural resources. They are what the civilisation wished them to be. There is, after all, far more expression of the human will in a traditional Chinese or Japanese house than in a modern American home. The latter is much better 'adapted' to the climate, for it is centrally heated in winter and air-conditioned in summer; it also comes closer to an economically rational use of resources since it uses materials that are not imposed by tradition but selected for convenience and cheapness.

Built with great care and restraint, peasant houses were stable and durable, and were kept in repair for a long time before being reconstructed on the same spot. The builder of a house was usually dead long before it needed rebuilding. Peasant houses, in respect of their dimensions, the care expended on their construction, and their total cost (bearing in mind that much of the work had been done by specialists), were often very much better than

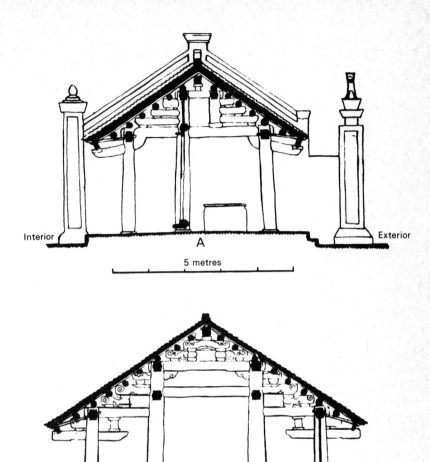

Interior   A   Exterior

5 metres

B

Fig. 14.1   The 'Le' temple at Thanh Hoa, in North Vietnam (drawings by J. Inguimberty, 1934). Above, cross-section of the entrance gate; below, section of one of the side-buildings. These drawings show a good example of the building up of a roof by 'stacking' the wooden components; the same principle was adopted for domestic buildings (cf., Fig. 14.16)

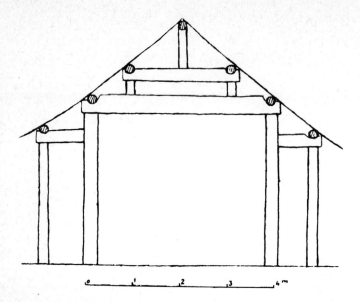

Fig. 14.2 Diagrammatic cross-section of a modern Chinese house (after Boerschmann, *Chinesische Architektur*, i, 61)

the poverty of the occupiers would have led one to expect. Many houses, indeed, reflected a higher degree of prosperity than that of the family occupying them; for when a peasant had amassed enough money, he hastened to build a beautiful house that would do credit to himself and give honourable shelter to the memorial plaques of his ancestors. After a reversal of fortune, or through the equal partitioning of a heritage, the inheritors of the property could fall back into poverty and yet continue to occupy a large and attractive house. There were thus many more elegant houses than well-to-do families. A Vietnamian proverb says that 'no family is rich for three generations, nor poor for three generations'; and the first part of this, at least, was certainly true.

HOUSES AND RELIGION

Houses in China, Japan and Vietnam are temples as well as residences. They shelter a living family, but the ancestral memorials

Fig. 14.3 Building a mud wall (from Hommel, 289). Based on a dry-stone wall, the layers of mud are tamped in a wooden box that is progressively raised

Fig. 14.4   A Chinese timber-frame house (after Hommel, 276). This drawing shows clearly the method of construction: the roof is finished before the
walls since it rests on the posts and not on the external walls. The framework is made of vertical columns, with horizontal beams and crown posts
supported by the beams

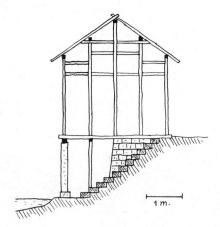

Fig. 14.5   A Chinese timber framework (after J. de Cholensky, Ninth Inter-
national Geographical Congress, Geneva, 1908. iii, 44). This drawing shows
the characteristic features of the framework, and also the adaptation of it to
changes in river level (on the banks of the Yangtse); in effect this is a
Chinese house built on poles and masonry

Fig. 14.6   A more elaborate Chinese timber framework (after R. Kelling, *Das Chinesische Wohnhaus*, 1935, 27; Kelling took the illustration from Li Ming Chung, *Construction in the Song Period*, 3 vols (in Chinese), Shanghai, 1912, 1923, 1929)

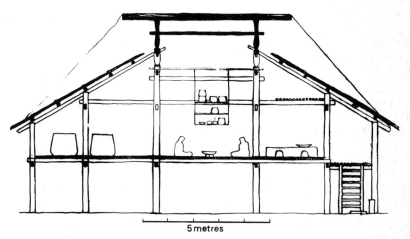

5 metres

Fig. 14.7   Section of a 'tho' house, built on poles, near Bac Kan, North Vietnam (drawing by J. Inguimberty)

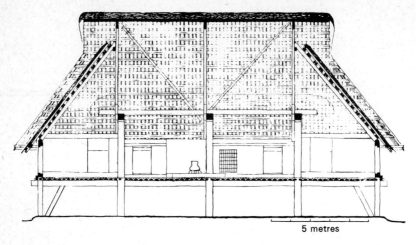

Fig. 14.8   Longitudinal section through an attractive 'muong' house, built on poles near Phu Nho Quan, in North Vietnam (drawing by J. Inguimberty)

are on the altar and the domestic deities lurk in the corners. The construction of a house thus had its religious as well as its technical aspects; and moreover, the structure of a private house did not differ from that of a temple (Fig. 14.1). A characteristic house was a multiple temple. For example, on entering a Vietnamese house in which the rites were dutifully observed, one would find on the right a small wooden recess dedicated to the Virgin mother of the West, but perhaps one would also see in her the goddess of feminine destiny. There were numerous deities to whom, on certain days, the woman of the house would offer incense or libations of pure water: as well as the ancestors, the 'genie' of the kitchen, and numerous other spirits concerned in the construction of the house. This example gives a good idea of the burden of religious preoccupations attaching to the house.

BUILDING MATERIALS OF VEGETABLE ORIGIN

From Cape Cambodia in the south to Hokkaido, the northernmost island of Japan, rural houses, though varied in detail, had essential characteristics in common. In the first place, they were

Fig. 14.9 Houses with enclosed courtyards, in northern China during winter with a very cold wind blowing (from an 1881 edition of Shu King)

built almost entirely of vegetable materials: the framework and
the supporting pillars were of wood, and the roof was thatched.
Most villages, viewed from a neighbouring height, appeared as a
uniform collection of thatched cottages, with no single building
raising its head above the general level of greyish straw. The great
Chinese treatise on architecture by Ying-tsao fa-che, of the
twelfth century, is primarily concerned with wooden structures.
All important buildings were described as 'great undertakings in
earth and wood'.

The desire to get large timbers to build imperial palaces was
responsible for deforesting many a Chinese mountain. In course
of time, the only remaining exploitable forests were limited to
remote districts in the western mountains; the local inhabitants
were dragooned into forced labour in these highlands, which
were greatly feared by the Chinese peasants. There was a popular
saying in Szechwan in the fifteenth century that ran thus: 'A
thousand go seeking timber in the mountains, but only five
hundred return.' We must not seek to explain the deforestation
of China solely by the use of timber in building, however, for
other factors were involved. Although the Nipponese were even
more addicted to building in wood than the Chinese, Japan was
not deforested.

After the twelfth century it became necessary to import
Japanese timber for imperial buildings. Japanese monks made
gifts of timber to Buddhist monasteries in China for the recon-
struction of pagodas. The explanation of the differences in the
appearance of the landscape in China and in Japan is to be found
in rules and regulations, effectively administered, that protected
Japanese forests, while there was no such control of forest in
China.

Exterior walls are of various materials, planks, bamboo trellis,
wattle-and-daub, unfired bricks, cob (Fig. 14.3), or baked bricks.
The walls simply enclose the house and do not support the roof,
which simply rests on the framework of poles. Even in southern
China, where the walls are of baked bricks and the roofs are tiled,
the weight of the roof is carried by the wooden framework.
Rural houses never show any signs of a generous and sensible use
of either stone or brick.

Another mark of this vegetable civilisation is that the frameworks are assembled by tenons and mortises, with no nails, screws, nuts or bolts. Such frameworks are just as easy to take down as to erect. In Vietnam, a needy landowner could actually sell his house while retaining the land on which it had stood. During troublous times, anxious peasants would dismantle their houses and dump the beams in the pond, thus avoiding the risks of incendiarism in the village.

It is not possible to find an explanation of this preference for vegetable materials in the natural conditions. China abounds in building stones; the Yangtse area and southern China have an abundance of limestone suitable for masonry, while the proximity of limestone and easily workable coal would, and do, permit the production of lime and cement. Elsewhere, the abundance of granite, slates, sandstones, clays, and coal for firing the bricks, offered every opportunity for building solid edifices in which the timber framework was reduced to a minimum or even avoided entirely by the construction of arches and domes. It is clear that the preference for vegetable materials is part of the civilisation. Perhaps it was an aesthetic preference. Why not, for what is an aesthetic preference but a mark of civilisation? In their traditional aspect these wooden houses had a charm that was not lost on their peasant occupiers.

It is to be feared that these traditional rural houses will disappear, to be replaced progressively by dwellings made from prefabricated parts in which concrete and corrugated sheeting are dominant. If this happens, the beauty of the countrysides will suffer; we can only hope that, in compensation, the new houses will be more comfortable than the rather incommodious traditional ones.

THE WOODEN FRAMEWORK

The structure of Far Eastern houses is thus conditioned by their timber framework, which consists of the columns that support the roof frame. The timberwork is erected before the walls; only one principle is involved, for all the columns are vertical and all the beams horizontal; there are no diagonals, no X-structures. Vertical crown posts and the main rafters control the slope of the roof (Figs. 14.2 and 14.4).

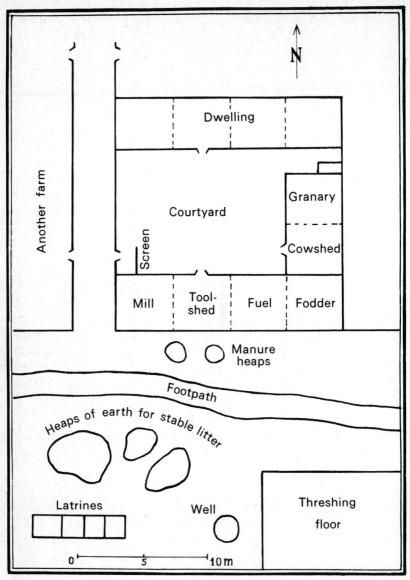

Fig. 14.10   A well-to-do farm in Hopeh province (after J. L. Buck, *Chinese Farm Economy*, 1930, 30). The dwelling faces south; the courtyard is enclosed, and a screen lies across the entrance; the well is adjacent to the latrines; the number and size of the outbuildings is an indication of the wealth of the landowner

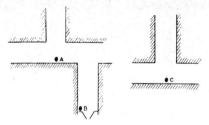

Fig. 14.11 'Stone dogs', in the streets of Dinh Bang village in the Red River delta. Dogs A and C obstruct harmful influences that come along the straight road; dog B protects the entrance to a house

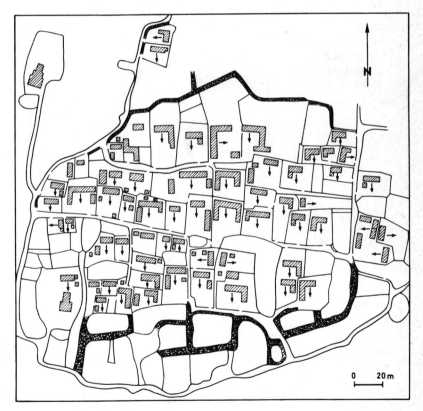

Fig. 14.12 South-facing houses, in the village of Phuong Vy, in the Red River delta. Arrows indicate the facade of the main dwellings, most of which face south. The shaded belts are bamboo hedges

Fig. 14.13 Troglodyte dwellings in Shensi, northern China (from Castell, 93). Here the houses are excavated in the side of a hill, not at the bottom of a pit. They are accompanied by normal houses

The size of the house is fixed by the length of the main beam, which is a single timber controlling the dimensions of the roof-truss. The houses are narrow, only 3 or 4 metres wide, despite the use of a device that, by permitting the tension of the main rafters at a lower angle of slope, makes it possible to enlarge the roof to a certain extent. Such timber frameworks are somewhat irrational for the beams, instead of being stressed only lengthwise, occasionally support upright posts that exert a vertical pressure on them (Figs. 14.5 and 14.6). This being so, the beams have to be of sufficient diameter to resist such pressure; if the stress had been in one direction only they could have been made smaller.

One explanation for the form of the Chinese house-framework has been suggested; it is that techniques originally necessitated by the employment of bamboo continued to be used after the substitution of timber. Bamboo, indeed, is very difficult to build up into any kind of framework involving diagonals or X-structures. But this is pure speculation.

These timber-framed houses, that did not make rational use of the possibilities of timber construction, were, at least in the wealthier examples, very pleasant in appearance. Their construction required great experience and respect for the traditional rules, and the result was a harmonious assemblage. Certainly there was none of that rather arid baldness that characterises the timber-framed buildings of the Western world. In Chinese and Vietnamian houses the rooms have no ceilings, so that the timbers are visible; on looking upwards, one's gaze is lost in the perspectives of parallel beams, all alike; and in the houses of the wealthier classes the posts, beams and cross-ties would be richly carved (though it must be acknowledged that such decorated roof timbers are great dust-collectors).

Chinese and Vietnamian houses are built flush with the ground; their posts rest on stone slabs that prevent the rise of moisture that would quickly rot the timber. The floors of the rooms are of beaten earth, or in wealthier houses, paved with squares of baked clay. Japanese houses have floors of wood, resting on small piles. Quite different are the houses of the mountain peoples of southwest China and Vietnam, for these are built on poles (Figs. 14.7 and 14.8). This, too, is an expression

Fig. 14.14   A landscape in the loess region, in the west of Honan province, near the Shensi border, close to Tong Kwan (from Castell, *Chinaflug*, 1938, 85). The peasants have utilised completely this piedmont slope, either in strip fields or in terraces. Unfortunately the loess is deeply dissected by gulleys and ravines that are continually enlarging at the expense of the cultivated fields. In the centre is a hamlet of troglodyte dwellings (see Fig. 14.15 for details)

of the way of life, for it is impossible to have recourse to explanations based on slope or the danger of flooding. Indeed, the Miao, who inhabit the most mountainous regions of southwestern China and Vietnam, build their houses on the ground, just like the Chinese of the lowest and most amphibious parts of the Yangtse delta. The ordinary house framework is intended only for single-storey buildings; but in Fukien the houses are much taller, with an upper storey that acts as a grain store.

The erection of the timber framework was accompanied by many subtle rites: in effect it was a religious ceremony as well as an architectural operation. Such rites varied from one region to another: in Tonkin, once the site had been chosen, an expert was

Fig. 14.15 Troglodyte dwellings in Honan province, northern China (from Castell, 85). Houses excavated in the loess, leading off from the side of a square pit. Access to the central courtyard is by a ramp, the entrance to which is seen in the drawing. Also in the picture are straw ricks

consulted, who would determine the most favourable date for the construction, based on astrological indications from the date of birth of the future owner of the house. The owner would then recruit carpenters, who would be treated with the greatest respect because they could so easily cast an evil spell over the house. If an ill-intentioned carpenter were to place inside a mortise a charm on which he had inscribed curses, the house would be haunted, and the owner would be awakened every night by these imprecations. To break the spell, the charm must be found, and this could only be done by the carpenter's chisel: for this reason the owner carefully preserved the chisel after the completion of the building.

Before commencing work, the master carpenter proceeded to mark out the timber, making himself a measuring rod. On this

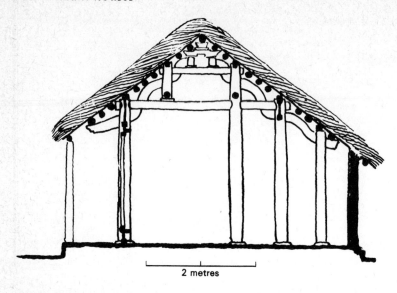

2 metres

Fig. 14.16 **Cross-section of a thatched timber-frame house, at Thanh Hoa, in North Vietnam (drawing by J. Inguimberty). The posts leave only narrow free spaces inside the house. Roof-timber construction resembles that of a 'Le' temple**

occasion the owner would make a sacrifice to the 'genie' of the carpenters, with sticky rice, pig's head and alcohol; naturally enough, the carpenters regaled themselves with these offerings. With the arrival of the appointed day, the next ceremony would be the erection of the principal beam, a longitudinal timber that formed the summit of the roof; placed on two bamboo trestles, this fixed the height of the house. Then the framework was built up from ground level until it reached the main beam. With the completion of the work, another feast followed. The measuring rod that had been used in the construction would be carefully placed underneath the roof beam, there to remain to protect the house from collapsing.

SITE ORIENTATION AND PLAN

The various parts of a dwelling are joined so as to form a hollow square (Fig. 14.9), but they are separate and there is no direct

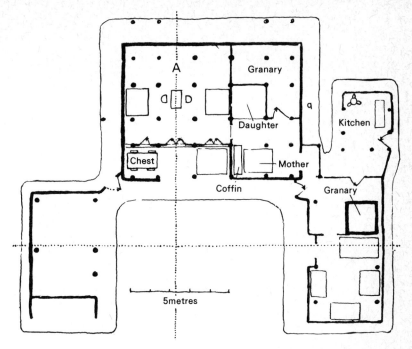

Fig. 14.17 The house at My Hoa (Fig. 14.19). Plan of the house, showing the ancestral altar (A); the fireproof grain store is in one of the lateral buildings

communication between them. The only entrance is placed, not in the wall of the house but in the wall that surrounds the court-yard; and it does not face the main building but leads through one of the lateral walls (Fig. 14.10). If, by reason of the layout, it was impossible to avoid placing the entrance opposite the main portion of the house, the path leading to the latter would be sharply curved, with screens placed between the entrance and the house (Fig. 14.22). These precautions were to keep out evil in-fluences that, being able to move only in straight lines, would be stopped by obstacles. With the same objective in mind, the peasants placed terrifying objects at the entrance, such as stone dogs, or clashing cowbells.

The desire to guard against evil spirits also played an important part in the siting of houses. Certain spots were considered unfit for habitation, for supernatural reasons, and they remained

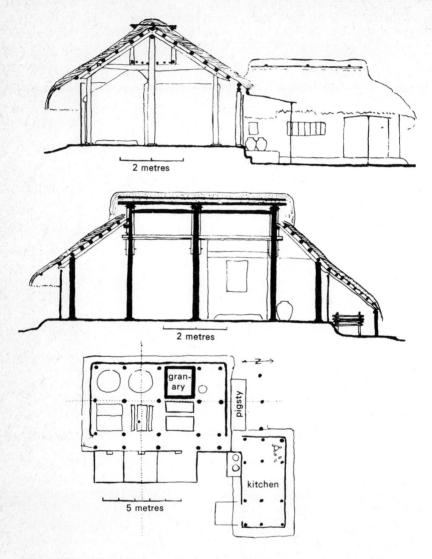

Fig. 14.18 A house built with axial columns and an internal fireproof granary, near Cua Tung, in Quang Tri province of North Vietnam (drawings by J. Inguimberty, 1934). The upper drawing is a transverse section showing the axial column (the granary, built of fireproof clay, can be seen on the left; note also the method of fixing the thatch, on the roofcrest); in the centre, a longitudinal section; at the bottom, the house in plan

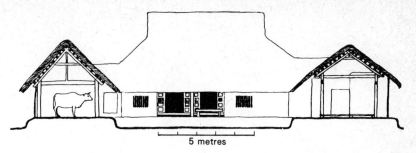

Fig. 14.19 A house with double roof and granary at My Hoa, in Binh Dinh province, Vietnam. A general view of the central building, with the lateral buildings shown in cross-section

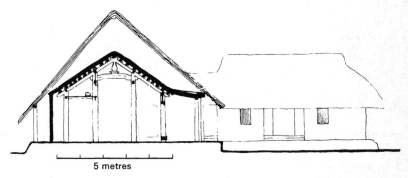

Fig. 14.20 The house at My Hoa (Figs. 14.19 and 14.17). Cross-section of the main building, showing the 'false roof' of clay and the outer thatched roof. (Figs. 14.17, 14.19 and 14.20 by J. Inguimberty, 1934)

empty of buildings; they could represent the back of the Earth Dragon. The front of the house must not be crossed by a straight line prolonging the course of a canal or a road, neither must it be 'threatened' by the angle of another house. If it was impossible to avoid such harmful threats, they would be warded off by magical mirrors or stone dogs (Fig. 14.11).

Houses usually faced south; in this instance the requirements of comfort and magic fortunately coincided. For the Chinese and neighbouring peoples, the North was feminine, corresponding to the Yin in the binomial Yin-Yang, and exercised a bad and debilitating influence. The South was masculine, the Yang, with a fertilising and enriching influence. Besides, the north winds of

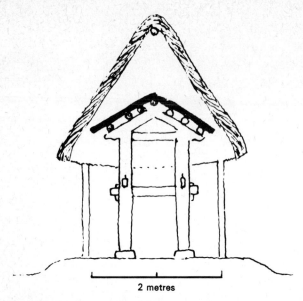

Fig. 14.21　Sketch of a small shrine at Binh Dinh, in Vietnam. A 'false roof' of clay and an outer roof of thatch

winter are strong and very cold, and it is desirable to shelter from them, whereas in summer the refreshing southerly breezes are welcomed with pleasure (Fig. 14.12).

The rural dwelling often contained more than one building. Alongside the main building, and at right angles to it, another would be erected on the same constructional principles. It could be used as a dwelling, but might also house the draught-oxen or buffaloes, and agricultural implements — but these latter, being neither large nor numerous, did not require much space.

LACK OF COMFORT

The traditional houses would appear to contain but little comfort. They are cold in winter — why, we shall see in a moment. They are badly aired in summer, because the end walls are windowless; and they are dark when the doors are closed. Cluttered up with the timber framework, they have but restricted floor space and contain many corners where insects and mice can shelter. These characteristics are less due to the poverty of the inhabitants than to custom, for the level of comfort does not rise with an increase in wealth. A poor house and a rich house might differ quite remarkably in size and in the quality of the building materials; the rich house would be much larger, would consist of a series of buildings separated by courtyards, would be built of costly woods, with high quality bricks and tiles. The construction of the beams would be more expert, giving that impression of strength and weight that contributed so much to the beauty of Chinese timber-frame houses. But this rich house would have just as many draughts in winter, and would be no better lit than the dwelling of a poor peasant.

The houses are difficult to close securely, for the doors are locked by simple latches that are easy to open. It is easy to force a window-entry, by simply pushing a hole through the walls made of wattle-and-daub or mud brick, easier still if the wall is of bamboo.

CHINESE HOUSES

The external appearance of Chinese houses varies from region to region. In the north, the walls are of mud brick (Fig. 14.3) or adobe, with a thatched roof (and in Kansu, the roofs are stepped as in central Asia). In the centre and south, walls are of baked brick with tiled roofs; this gives a much better and more solid appearance, but is more expensive. The mud walls of the northern houses have but little strength; rising damp erodes them, despite the precautions that are taken such as brick foundations covered with a damp course of reeds, and alkaline waters in particular deposit salts that cause the walls to crumble. True, the destruction of the walls does not necessarily lead to the ruination of the whole house, for the roof is supported by the timber framework, and the walls can be quickly refashioned. But broken walls are a nuisance and reduce still further the degree of comfort inside the house.

The provinces of Honan and Shensi contain more troglodytes than anywhere else in the world. The loess formation lends itself admirably to the excavation of underground dwellings; a simple hoe suffices to scrape out rooms and passages; the walls do not disintegrate and are not damp. There are two types of such dwellings, those on the flanks of a hillside (Fig. 14.13), and those arranged around a deep square pit that is connected to the surface by a ramp (Figs. 14.14 and 14.15). These troglodyte houses are much pleasanter than the ordinary houses of Shensi. They are less cold in winter, and cooler in summer. They need no timber for building — and in any case wood is scarce in northern China. One undoubted inconvenience is the liability of the area to earthquakes; this is a zone of tectonic contact between the fault-bounded Tsinling mountain range and the uplifted block of Shansi. Seismic shocks can bury whole communities, but the danger does not seem to discourage the population, which numbers its troglodytes in millions.

Chinese houses were badly lit; windows were few and small, just openings, with wooden bars, and neither glass nor shutters. In winter, they were covered by paper, giving no ventilation and but little light; if it were necessary to see what was going on outside, without opening the door and letting in an icy blast, a moistened finger could poke a hole in the paper.

Peasant houses in the area north of northern Kiangsu used an efficient system of heating; it is perhaps surprising, as we shall see, that the Japanese had no real means of heating, but it is even more surprising that China, south of the southern part of Kiangsu, should have been deprived of winter heating, bearing in mind that in Nanking January is as cold as in Paris. The matter of heating clearly divides China into two parts, the north and the south (the latter including the Yangtse region).

The means of heating is the *k'ang*. Like the Korean *ondol*, this is a large stove built of crude brickwork. It is heated by hot air from the adjacent kitchen fire. The kitchen fireplace is also made of crude bricks; it supports a hemispherical cooking-pot made of thin cast iron. The pot is used for all sorts of cooking: soups, rice, meat, even frying. While the food is cooking in the pot, a bamboo tray can be placed on top of it, containing a plate with other foodstuffs, and the whole covered by a kind of upturned bucket.

The object of all this is to economise on fuel. Over the greater part of China, the only fuel available for cooking and heating is

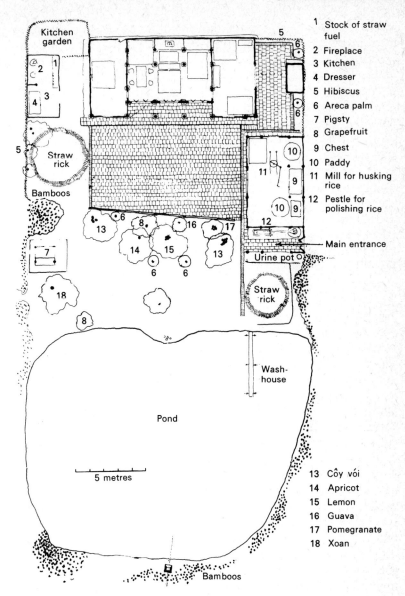

Key:

1 Stock of straw fuel
2 Fireplace
3 Kitchen
4 Dresser
5 Hibiscus
6 Areca palm
7 Pigsty
8 Grapefruit
9 Chest
10 Paddy
11 Mill for husking rice
12 Pestle for polishing rice

Main entrance

13 Côy vói
14 Apricot
15 Lemon
16 Guava
17 Pomegranate
18 Xoan

Urine pot

Wash-house

Pond

5 metres

Bamboos

Fig. 14.22 Plan of a large house in the suburbs of Hanoi, in North Vietnam (drawing by J. Inguimberty)

straw. The bitter winter in the north is indeed terrible for the peasants, with such a dearth of fuel. A little hot air in the k'ang was the only relief from the intense cold; the k'ang is like a mother, say the peasants.

After three or four years the k'ang would be worn out; its dry bricks would be cracked, and smoke would leak out. Another one must be built. Fortunately the broken mudbricks are full of soot, and form an excellent fertiliser, rich in potash, phosphorus and nitrogen.

In the rural areas of China the use of foot-warmers was common. These, for hands as well as feet, consisted of a bamboo framework containing a pot filled with live charcoal. Similarly, there were seat-warmers consisting of a wooden cylinder with a clay brazier inside; these were used especially by old ladies who sat on them while protecting vegetables in the process of drying from being devoured by voracious pigs, dogs and fowls.

THE HOUSES OF VIETNAM

Vietnamian houses (Fig. 14.23) bear a strong resemblance to those of China; for the most part they are timber-framed and built directly on the ground (Fig. 14.16). The frameworks consist mainly of vertical posts; the walls are of wattle-and-daub, puddled clay, or bamboo trellis, and the main house is accompanied by other buildings that surround an enclosed courtyard (Fig. 14.22).

The central part of the main building contains the ancestral altar; this room is also the reception room and the male quarters. The floor space, interrupted by the wooden posts of the framework, is almost entirely occupied by beds, made of wooden planks resting on trestles, and by the altar, the red and gold lacquer of which shines in the semidarkness. A screen across the entrance door prevents the altar from being seen from the courtyard, so the room is gloomy. The head of the family sleeps close to the memorial tablets, does homage to them, clothed in a black muslin tunic and wearing a turban of the same material; here also he receives visitors and invites them to take a cup of tea, smoke his waterpipe and spit in the shining copper spittoon. The floor is

Fig. 14.23   Types of roof in the Red River delta: Nos 1 to 7, thatched roofs; 8 and 9, tiled roofs (drawing by J. Inguimberty)

of beaten earth, or baked clay paving blocks. Chickens and dogs wander around freely; the visitor must beware of the dog lying concealed under a bed. The decoration is made up of parallel devices in gold Chinese characters on a black lacquer background.

On each side of the main room is a smaller room, two small nooks with no openings other than the door leading to the main room, and no light save that which filters through the roof and the walls. Here the women sleep, and here too are stored the large baskets and earthenware jars that contain grain.

It is rare for any precautions to be taken against fire; only the richest landowners built granaries of puddled clay outside their houses. However, in central Annam, the peasants guard against fire either by fitting up a kind of fireproof chest in the house (it is made of beaten earth and is called a *nha ruong*, or house chest), or by constructing underneath the thatched roof a false roof of clay to protect the house if the thatch should catch fire. In the latter case the main timber framework is underneath the clay roof; the thatch is supported by an independent and much lighter frame (Figs. 14.18 and 14.19). This type of house is locally known as *nha thuong ruong ha roi*, the upper part being of *ruong* type, the lower part *roi*. The *roi* house, in central Annam, is characterised by a roof truss that has a central beam on the longitudinal axis of the house (Figs. 14.17 and 14.20). The anti-fire technique has become so ingrained that even isolated altars, though they are at no risk, are provided with two roofs, one of clay and one of thatch (Fig. 14.21). These constructions remind one very much of the fireproof shelters that the Japanese build alongside their houses; and it is not without interest to recall that Japanese were very frequent visitors to the harbour of Tourane (Da Nang) in the early seventeenth century.

The kitchen is placed outside the principal building, and opens only on to the courtyard (in China and Japan it is not separated from the dwelling). The cooking apparatus is more rudimentary than in Chinese houses, for whereas in the latter cooking is done on a stove the top of which accommodates a cast iron pot of hemispherical shape, the arrangement in Vietnam consists of no more than three brick supports on which the rice-boiling pot rests. Boiling water under these conditions requires a great deal of patience; the operator must sit for long periods on his heels, feeding the fire under the pot with straw. The kitchen would contain but few utensils: several basins, a few sticks, a water jar with a ladle made from a coconut shell with a bamboo handle.

The building containing the kitchen is placed at right angles to the main building; it is constructed on the same principles but with less care. It may also contain a stable for a buffalo or a draught ox, a recess for storing implements, and a second reception room of lower grade than the one in the main building. Sometimes there may also be a coffin, given in a spirit of filial piety by the son to the father, who can thus constantly admire it and meditate on the beauty of his last resting place.

A pigsty enclosed by strong wooden bars, was generally found in close proximity to the house. If the peasant had any fodder, he would keep the pigs confined in order to conserve their droppings, which were regarded as an excellent fertiliser. The pigsty was usually constructed using planks from an old coffin, for this wood possessed properties that would protect the pigs from evil influences. It was a custom in Vietnam to exhume corpses several years after burial; the bones were then placed in an earthenware jar and reburied.

All the buildings open on to a courtyard garden; they have no outside doors. On the side of the courtyard opposite the ancestral altar, a stone screen prevents the access of evil spirits. Beyond this screen is a small garden, adorned by several areca palms; this most elegant of palm trees, with its surprisingly thin trunk and its dense plume of leaves, would often be entwined by a betel liana, and the union of these two useful plants represented for the Vietnamese a touching symbol of conjugal fidelity. Other plants in the garden might include fruit trees such as citron, mandarin, guava, jack-fruit, grapefruit, mangoes, bananas, mangosteen, a few tea bushes (the green leaves of which would be used for making tea), and some vegetables. The entrance to the garden is often sheltered by a small 'house' with a timber framework and pitched roof. In the courtyard is a small astrological altar. If the garden ends in a pond, the household thus has the last word in convenience: a floating plank projecting from the edge, a ladle to scoop up the water — and the bathroom is complete. At the same time the pond acts as a sink for washing the dishes, cleaning vegetables and washing clothes. The pond serves all domestic needs for water except for drinking; for this there is a tank or a well. Finally, it contains fish, and duckweed that can be used to feed the pigs (Fig. 14.22).

Though the essential characteristics of the Vietnamian house were the same throughout the country, there were regional variations. A closer study in the area between Than Hoa in the north and Binh Dinh in the south reveals no less than seven peasant house types, each localised in one of the small plains that are strung out along the Annamese coast. The types are Than Hoa, Vinh, Ha Tinh, Huong Khe (the most striking feature of which is the number of houses provided with a loft that almost amounts to a second storey), Rou (with Quang Tri and Hue) (a type having a central pillar and a false roof of clay), Quang Nam (including houses with a double roof of clay and thatch), and Binh Dinh (houses with a very high roof, a large space being enclosed between the clay roof and the thatched roof) (Figs. 14.17, 14.19 and 14.20).

These Vietnamian houses usually had charm; the drab colours of the walls and roofs blended pleasantly with the intense green of the trees. True, they lacked modern comforts, but the peasants dwelt in a peaceful and harmonious atmosphere.

JAPANESE HOUSES

In Japan, ancient rural house types have been carefully preserved right up to modern times; but changes are not taking place with great rapidity. We now see roofs of corrugated sheet steel, looking ugly when new and no better when rusty, glistening after a shower of rain, instead of thatch. But it remains true that the art of thatching, almost forgotten in Europe, is still held in some esteem in Japan (Figs. 14.25 and 14.26).

Like other houses in the Far East, the Japanese dwelling is made from vegetable materials and rests directly on the ground. There are no foundations; the columns that support the timber framework rest on stone blocks. The house is thus, in effect, built on low piles, with the floor about 50 cm above ground level. This arrangement, so different from the Chinese house, would appear to indicate that the Japanese house type is of

Indonesian origin. It is not, however, easy to see what advantage accrues from this suspended flooring, because it is impossible to do anything with the space underneath it. Was it for health reasons? Probably not; more likely just a tradition, a custom.

The timber framework of private houses is built on the same principles as those already discussed. It has been suggested that construction in easily-dismantled vegetable materials was very appropriate in a land subject to frequent and sometimes violent earthquakes. At first sight this seems plausible. But unfortunately the Japanese framework has the disadvantage of being top-heavy, and this can be very dangerous if it collapses.

The traditional houses were unostentatious in appearance; the visible timbers were weather-stained, the thatch had lost its colour through rainwash, and no paint protected the woodwork or enlivened the generally dull hues. Occasionally, as in the plain north of Tokyo, a splash of colour would appear: here the houses had a flat rooftop covered with flowers — red lilies, white or purple irises, varying from village to village. Viewed from a neighbouring hill such villages presented a strange and delightful picture, with their dull grey roofs crowned by bright colours. The treatment of this roof crown, the most delicate part of the whole thatch, and most liable to leaks, varied widely; at least fifteen types were recognisable, each characteristic of its own small region.

Japanese houses are open to both sun and wind; in fact two or three of the four external walls are made of movable panels that are raised each morning. Thus the Japanese can be in the open air whilst remaining in the house. Sliding partitions enable the separate rooms to be thrown into one large room. The interior of the house is tastefully furnished. Even in the rural areas the *ramma*, that is the space between the door-lintel and the ceiling, is decorated with geometrical or stylised floristic designs. The plan of the house is not as symmetrical as in China or Vietnam,

The Japanese house is distinguished by its meticulous cleanliness. The wooden floors are polished until they look like marble, and in order not to tarnish them, the peasants remove their shoes on entering. The rooms are small and unencumbered: there are no beds, nor tables, nor chairs. Indispensable objects are placed in cupboards. The people sleep on the floor, on cotton quilts that

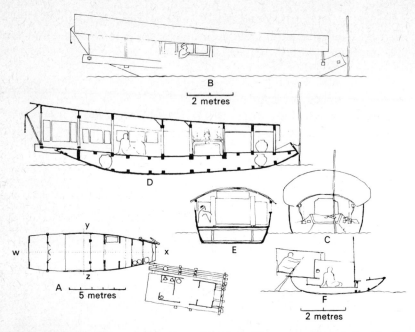

Fig. 14.24 Houseboat types in a floating village near Hanoi, in North Vietnam (drawings by J. Inguimberty). A, plan of a large wooden sampan, with ancestral altar, and an accompanying kitchen-raft; B, longitudinal view of this sampan; C, view of the prow; D, longitudinal section of the sampan; E, cross-section of the sampan; F, a small sampan made of plaited bamboo, used for passenger transport

are stowed away during the daytime. The peasants bathe at least once a day; the bathroom is often accessible from outside, so that the hot bathwater can be used not only by the inhabitants of the house but also by neighbours, thus saving fuel.

The kitchen is under the same roof as the rest of the house, but is at a slightly lower level, being directly on the ground. Fuel is used rather less economically than in China, for the hot-water-bottle or cooking pot is simply placed on a tripod. The smoke goes where it will, for there is no chimney. It escapes through the thatch, which at certain times of the day looks as if it is on fire. Fires, indeed, are frequent, and the Japanese peasants used to live in constant fear of a conflagration. In order to limit the damage, they would build, at some distance from the house, a grain-store

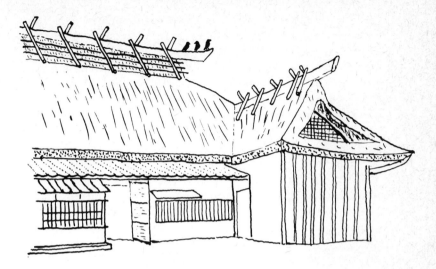

Fig. 14.25   Part of a well-to-do family house at Kabutoyama, in Musashi province, Japan (from Morse, *Japanese Homes*, London, 1880, 62)

Fig. 14.26   Japanese houses: a village street at Nagaike, Yamushiro (from Morse, 72)

and a *kura*, a fireproof shelter built of earth, in which to keep their most precious possessions. The Japanese house is but poorly adapted to the climate. The winters in Japan are cold (see p. 14), but no serious attempt is made to combat low temperatures. Although much cleaner and more comely than the Chinese house, the Japanese dwelling is less comfortable in winter than the houses of northern China; they have nothing comparable with the Chinese k'ang (p. 192). Besides, how is it possible to heat a house that is always open to the wind during the day? Even at night, the sliding panels made of stretched paper provide little protection from cold draughts. The Japanese warm themselves by taking very hot baths and donning knitted undergarments; and when they are really too cold, they warm their hands over a brazier. This is a complicated and dangerous arrangement; they place a pan containing burning charcoal in a specially made depression in the floor, sit around it with their legs extended, and place over the brazier a metal framework covered with a quilt, to conserve the hot air. It is unsatisfactory and very liable to start a fire.

CHAPTER 15

THE VILLAGE FRAMEWORK

He who makes virtue the main stem of his
government may be compared to the pole star that
stays immobile while all the other stars revolve
around it.

Confucius

A CONCENTRATED RURAL HABITAT

In China and in Vietnam the villages have names that are of little
geographical significance (Fig. 15.7); both village and regional
toponymy are characterised by clichés and literary allusions. The
name of the large alluvial island of Tsong Ming, at the mouth of
the Yangtse, means 'respect for intellectual faculties'; this has
nothing whatever to do with the nature of the island, or with its
relatively recent history of colonisation, less still with the rustic
reputation of its inhabitants.

As a general rule, the dwellings of a community are grouped in
villages and hamlets; isolated houses are rare, and only to be
found in parts of Szechwan, Honan, Kiangsu (for example on the
island of Tsong Ming) and in Japan. A remarkable example from
Japan is the dispersed settlement of the Satsuma country in the
south of Kyushu island; here the separate houses are sited on
valley slopes without being collected into villages, and it is noteworthy that in the case of large valleys oriented east—west the
dwellings seek the north-facing slope, the shady side; the reason
for this is the desire for protection from the typhoon winds,
which blow from the south. The nucleation of rural houses in the
Far East is not due to the rarity of water sources; it occurs
equally in areas with abundant fresh water supplies as in more
arid areas, and is just one of the traditions of the civilisation.

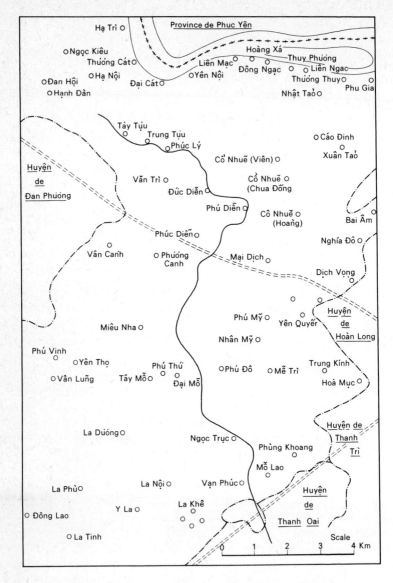

Fig. 15.1   Place-names in part of the Red River delta in Vietnam

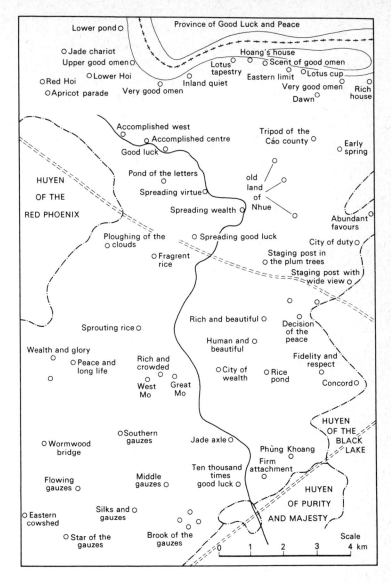

Fig. 15.2 Translation of the place-names shown in Fig. 15.1. The object of this translation is to show that the toponymy has little geographical significance; it is of literary interest only. Exceptions are the village names containing the word 'la' (= gauze or veil), referring to the weaving of silk cloth

The institutions that regulate peasant life within a rigid frame-work function much better if the houses are concentrated in villages rather than being scattered over the countryside. But the Far Eastern village is not just a simple collection of family dwellings; its people are linked to each other by a common cult and by a feeling of solidarity. A peasant leaves his village with regret and will willingly return to it if he has been obliged to emigrate. Contrariwise, 'strangers' are unwelcome. It is true that the village has to accept many brides born elsewhere, since young men are commonly prohibited from marrying within the community. But life can be very difficult for a male 'stranger'; with no land, and excluded from the village institutions, he would be treated very coldly indeed. In Tonkin each village would commonly shelter one outsider, but one only; he would be a poor wight who, by reason of his lack of means, would accept all the degrading and dirty domestic jobs in the village that the inhabitants were un-willing to do themselves. In some ways the village was a sort of exclusive caste.

In Japan, a person expelled from his village could not enter another community; he became a *hinin* (a non-human being), an outlaw, existing by singing in the streets or begging.

The largest village seen by the author of this book numbered 18 000 souls. Even an agglomeration as large as this remained a village; the male inhabitants tilled the fields, and had been born in the village; the houses were all of rural type, and no part of the village had any urban aspect; it was a self-administered com-munity, not governed by the agents of a superior government organisation. A town might have many fewer people, but its inhabitants would have come from many different places, would not necessarily be permanently located there, and would have non-agriculture occupations; the houses, built in serried rows, and always with tiled roofs, were very different in aspect from those of a village.

Because of the high density of population, the villages are a more important part of the rural landscape; in the Red River delta they occupy 8 per cent of the total land surface. From almost any viewpoint in these Far Eastern plains, the horizon is ringed with villages. But as often as not the villages are concealed by a screen of trees, so that the effect is a mass of greenery rather

Fig. 15.3 Villages in the lower delta of the Red River. Scale 1/500 000.
This is an actual buildings-pattern map. Note the strings of settlement along
former beach lines, and signs of recent extension of the land into the sea

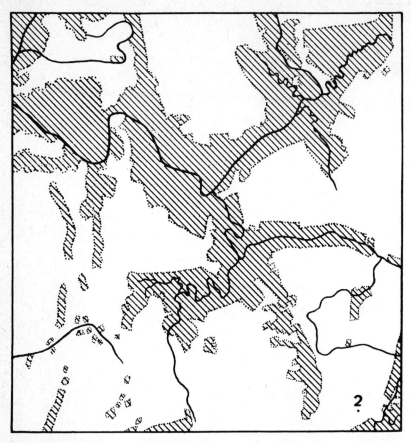

Fig. 15.4 Villages in the middle delta of the Mekong. Scale 1/100 000.
The area is 12 km west of Ben Tre (shown on the 1/100 000 map of the
Service Géographique de l'Indochine, sheet 235, Vinh Long). The villages
are aligned along the streams. They are strung out with but little nucleation.
They may occupy almost half the total area, but they enclose within their
perimeters many gardens and cultivated patches. One can hardly speak in
such a case of 'concentrated' population

than a collection of dwellings (Fig. 14.12).

The villages are not just randomly distributed. Their location is
a response to several needs: to be above flood level, to avoid the
most fertile and the most easily cultivated areas that are best
used for cropping, to respect the susceptibilities of the spirits of
the earth and air, as revealed by geomancy, and to conform to

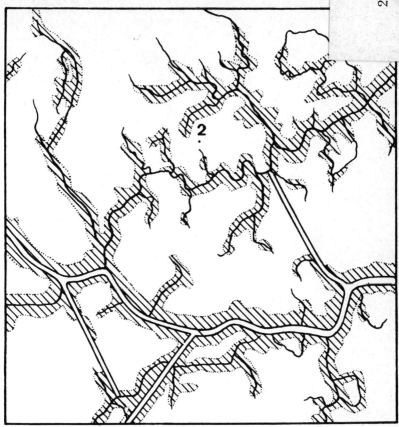

Fig. 15.5 Villages in the west of the Mekong delta. Scale 1/100 000. The area is 10 km west of Can Tho, shown on sheet 234 of the 1/100 000 map series. Villages aligned along the distributaries, but much narrower and less well developed than in the area shown on Fig. 15.4. This is an area of more recent and less dense settlement

development plans. The first two of these requirements explain the preference for slightly elevated localities; natural river levees, especially if reinforced by dykes, were used by long strings of villages, as in the province of Ha Dong in northern Vietnam, or the Echigo plain along the Shinano River in Japan. Isolated hills are ringed by villages, and if they are not malarial, the mountains that frame the plains offer village sites on the lower talus slopes; thus the north bank of Suwa lake, in Honshu, Japan, is studded

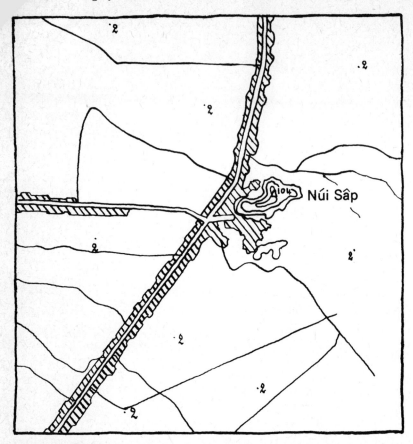

Fig. 15.6 Villages in the extreme west of the Mekong delta (on sheet 234 of the 1/100 000 map series). The village of Rach Gia is aligned along a canal. In this roadless country the houses line the canal banks, and the villages are very narrow; there are no longer rows of houses surrounded by gardens, along each bank. The hill of Nui Sap is the last of the line of NW–SE hills that parallel the lower Mekong from Takeo in Cambodia

with villages built on the alluvial fans of the torrents that come down from the mountains. Littoral dunes are lined by elongated villages whose locations trace the successive stages in the evolution of the strandlines along an emergent coast (Fig. 15.3). The streetvillages of the plain of Kwanto (Tokyo) are a response to the systematic subdivision of the land by strips at right angles to the roads. The square villages of the Kyoto plain bear witness to another system of land management, the *jori*, in which each village is placed in the centre of its square territory. The influence attributed to supernatural powers can sometimes be seen in discontinuities in the built-up area, discontinuities that are inexplicable by any physical attributes of the site (Figs. 15.4—7).

VILLAGE AUTONOMY

The village was usually very conscious of its identity, asserting its autonomy and only reluctantly allowing a higher authority to meddle in its affairs. Usually, moreover, the representatives of the state shared this viewpoint and preferred to deal not with individual citizens but with a village community that undertook to deal with all relations between individuals and the state, such as registration, tax collection, and army recruitment.

The village authorities thus had powers exceeding those of many Western municipalities. The village contrived to maintain this position, and gave a cold reception to the police force of the mandarins; these policemen were in any case usually rascals who were anxious to grind the faces of the villagers under any pretext. It was not unknown, in the old China, for policemen to be stoned. The possibility of such an incident was sufficient to make the mandarin very circumspect; for a mandarin could be forgiven anything except having allowed a riot to occur; a public disturbance would cause his removal from the district, if not his actual dismissal from office.

Self-sufficient, the village had few relations with its neighbours; but in China there were village leagues, formed to resist brigands. In Tonkin some villages were united by religious links, because they revered the same or related spirits. But on the other hand there were neighbouring villages that were separated by innumerable squabbles that sometimes degenerated into battles.

The villagers were at one in their worship of the local 'genie'. Each Japanese village had its *Ujigami*, or parish temple of Shintoism, for the worship of a deity that was usually the ancestor of the clan. Every Chinese village also had its temple dedicated to the local deity. In Vietnam, every non-Catholic village had a *dinh*, the temple of the local deity, as its most important building. The dinh was built on low piles, perhaps recalling a former period when the houses of the ancestors of the Vietnamian people (not yet truly Vietnamian, for the civilisation was not yet soaked in Chinese technology), like those of the Indonesians, were built on piles. Some village temples, built one or two centuries ago, were constructed with grace and magnificence; the dinh at Dinh Bang, in northern Vietnam, is a masterpiece of architecture in wood. In Japan, the statue of the local deity, or the mirror that represents it, shelters under a small temple linked by a covered way to a much larger building that houses the shrine of the deity and all the accessories that are brought out at festivals; the whole is surrounded by gardens in which there is an ancient sacred tree that was perhaps the origin of the cult; the sacred enclosure is entered by a monumental wooden gate.

The local legend of the deity often made him, in Vietnam as in China, a deified man, to whom the village owed the foundation of its craft. At the festivities given in honour of these deities the actions of the craft or industry were mimed; sometimes the legend had it that the profession was a dishonourable one (there were burglar deities), in which case the miming was done in secret.

The cult of the local genie demonstrated the unity of the village population and gave rise to much appreciated merry-making. Festivals were celebrated in honour of the genie, with theatrical performances, dances, wrestling, boat races, singing and banquets. In Japan, at the spring and autumn festivals, the young men performed a play before the villagers; Japanese peasants were indeed very interested in the theatre, both as actors and as spectators. When the spectators were carried away by the acting of one of the performers, they could not contain their enthusiasm, and with cries of joy, showered the stage with anything that came to hand; on the contrary they would hurl insults at the actor who displeased them. Every Nipponese village contained several families in which theatrical talent was hereditary. If it happened that a son of one of these families (for only males were allowed to perform) appeared to have no talent, the family would consider itself dishonoured; peasants have been known to

banish a son-in-law, married to their daughter, simply because he
was a bad actor. The intervals in the plays were very long, and a
performance might go on for twenty-four hours at a stretch; the
spectators would refresh themselves with sweets, and cakes made
of bean flour, purchased from perambulating salesmen, or relax
by playing party games.

In some Japanese villages the feasts given before the New Year
had a quality of mystical fervour that sheds a curious light on the
depths of the Nipponese character. Such is the flower-feast
(*hanamatsouri*) organised in isolated villages to the west of
Fujiyama. It all happens in front of the shrine of the local deity.
The dancers purify themselves by abstaining from meat, living
shut up in a house, and bathing in a sacred river. There is a
procession, with songs calling on the gods; then the dancers
begin, around a large cauldron filled with river water. The dances
go on all night, and then all the villagers, men and women, join in
the collective ecstasy; they go round and round the cauldron,
sprinkling each other with the water that it contains.

In China theatrical performances were also important, but
they were given by professional players and paid for by the
village. They took place in a temporary theatre constructed
outside the village, of bamboo and straw. Such performances
were organised as thanksgivings to the deities, so the village's
financial resources had to be in good order; but the generosity of
a rich person might help out the situation. The peasants were
passionately fond of these performances, and would invite all
their relatives from neighbouring villages. But these inevitable
invitations rather spoilt the peasants' pleasure, for all the guests
had to be fed, and this was an expensive matter. It was also
necessary to guard against thieves attracted by the crowds; one
member of the family must remain at home to protect the house
and prepare the meals. On the eve of a performance, the peasant
would kill his chickens so as to make sure they were not stolen.
Despite these unpleasantnesses the theatre was well received; it
would never have been invited if the economic situation had not
permitted the peasants to afford all the extra expenses. Hosts and
visitors gossiped all night, exchanging news of their little rural
world.

In Vietnam, among the numerous rites in the cult of the village deity, the most important was the feast for all the citizens, in front of the shrine. The people would be grouped at tables according to their age and their rank in the communal hierarchy. Such feasts aroused passionate interest, both for their gastronomic attraction and through the rivalries awakened by the seating arrangements.

The cult of the local genie was the only official village worship. But there existed many other cults, served by temples and altars. The Japanese village would have several places of worship, including a Buddhist pagoda. A Chinese or Vietnamian village, in addition to its temple for the local deity, might have a Buddhist pagoda, a temple of the arts, a temple of war, and numerous other smaller temples, as well as all the domestic altars. One Vietnamian village, for example, had places of worship for the following: the local deity, the arts, war, Buddha, the god of medicine, the three united saints (Confucius, Lao Tsu, Buddha), the spirit of the well, the spirit of the earth, the spirit of the trees and the spirit of the tiger.

VILLAGE CUSTOMS

The high population density of each village was made possible by an efficient administration, capable of maintaining harmonious relations within a very numerous body of people, of building up and maintaining such a group, and of facing the problem of increasing numbers.

Far Eastern villages were, in their own way, democratic communities in which birth gave no privileges. True, there were some inequalities between peasants, but higher status was linked with age, or with honours conferred by the state government. Rich and poor dressed alike, a fact which favoured the poor. In those parts of northern China where kaoliang (a tall sorghum) was cultivated, the lower leaves were torn off to hasten maturity. When the time came for this operation, all the inhabitants had the right to take part in the defoliation, in whatever field they pleased, and to use the leaves as fodder. The proprietor had no say in the matter, so long as the peasants did not take off leaves at a higher level than was the normal custom. In the same way, the authorities fixed the date for the beginning of gleaning in the cotton fields; from this date, anyone could glean anywhere, even though the harvest of bolls was not yet complete.

In Japan tradition and custom limited the power of wealth; so, in order not to excite hostility within the village, the richer people would not take advantage of all the rights that modern Japanese civil law accorded to landowners. In this way, by respecting local customs, they did not offend public opinion; but of course it meant some sacrifice on the part of the wealthier citizens.

Korean villages were distinguished from others in the Far East by the fact that they comprised an upper class (*yangban*) and a lower class (*sangnom*), with a marriage prohibition between them.

The possession or acquisition of wealth created difficulties for a rich villager. His fellow-citizens, who considered themselves his equals, and were as often as not related to him, overwhelmed him with requests for gifts of grain or money. It required a great deal of tact to avoid acceding to all these demands and giving offence to relatives whose solicitations were rejected — for these relatives would consider that they were entitled to share the wealth of their kinsman. Faced by these problems, the rich landowner might react by trying to secure political power — which he might do by his generosity to the village authorities and, by similar financial inducements, securing the approval of the mandarin administration. Alternatively, he might leave the village and instal an agent who had no power to make gifts or loans to the relatives. The administration of a rural fortune demanded great adroitness, for riches alone were insufficient to guarantee any authority within the village.

The common interest involved the exercise of collective restraints. The individual peasant was responsible for his actions to the village authorities, who could intervene if he disregarded the accepted customs — if, for example, he did not conduct himself as a good father, or a good son. The village acted as judge in family disputes, which were decided by public opinion in accordance with the custom. In Japan, at the festival of the local deity, the communal verdict would be announced and punishment inflicted for violations of the local morals. The shrine of the deity was carried on shoulders through the streets; preceded by dancers half drunk with saké, the deity would visit the citizens' houses. The procession would stop outside the dwellings of the guilty parties, then enter and ransack them. Such actions were against the law, but the peasant who opposed them or put in a complaint could not have continued to live in his native village.

The peasants were happy to belong to a group that controlled them, directed them, protected and assisted them, and in which they could exercise some influence. The villager lived within a framework that was uniform and active; he was not isolated, and found himself in agreement with the ideals of the community of which he formed a part.

Peasant solidarity was scarcely apparent in the field of agriculture; each peasant cultivated his own plot and could never count on any assistance from his neighbours since the times of most concentrated agricultural work were the same for all. If neighbours did sometimes assist, this was certainly not a general rule; the most likely time was at the replanting of the rice, for it is of considerable advantage to have this done very rapidly, so that the entire crop grows in a uniform fashion, all the plants have identical water requirements and all come to maturity at the same time. Much labour is therefore needed, and friends and neighbours find it mutually profitable to help each other. They can do this because, although the season for the replanting may be inescapable, the exact date can be fixed within certain limits. Those who receive help provide a meal for the helpers. At harvest time things are rather different; the ripe rice cannot wait, and everyone harvests for himself as rapidly as possible; if the household cannot provide sufficient labour for the business, the peasant must pay for hired labour, at rates that are the year's highest.

Some Chinese peasants grouped themselves together to irrigate their paddyfields. In those parts of Kiangsu province where a kind of biennial rotation was practised (first year, wheat followed by rice; second year wheat and soya), the farmers agreed to divide their lands into two sections, one devoted to each of these rotations; by this means it was much easier to irrigate the rice.

Village solidarity was expressed in the money contributions of people invited to funeral or marriage feasts, and in a great variety of other ways. One of the most widespread was the funeral association, in which the participants guaranteed each other suitable obsequies; the association possessed adequate funeral furniture, and the members would all follow the corpse of a dead colleague, thus assuring a dignified cortège. Korean villages had societies for the payment of taxes, for the maintenance of schools, for marriage expenses, and for the purchase of draught animals; those peasants who could not afford to buy an ox formed a club, to which they subscribed their small contributions. Lots were drawn each year to see who would scoop the pool; but village solidarity ensured that the lucky one would continue to pay his subscription until the club was wound up. There were several other sorts of subscription in the Far East. In Korean villages there were also purely recreational societies, old peoples' groups, and poetry clubs. Groups of this kind also existed throughout China. And there were others like the 'bowl clubs': several peasants would subscribe to purchase 200 or 300 fingerbowls, and would hire them out to organisers of funeral or marriage feasts; the fees would be divided among the subscribers. In the 'New Year friendly societies' the members paid a monthly subscription for the first five months of the year; the society then used the accumulated capital to grant loans at a low rate of interest. It dipped into its funds at harvest time and bought grain when the price was at its lowest; then sold it at the end of the year when the price was at its peak. The society then settled its accounts; with its capital and its profits it purchased cakes and cotton cloth for distribution among the members, who could thus feed and clothe themselves suitably to celebrate the New Year.

In the large villages of Tonkin the peasants were grouped in district associations, literary associations, groups of military mandarins, old peoples' clubs, wrestling clubs, societies of singers, of musicians, of traders, clubs for cock-fighting or for songbirds, or pupils of the same teacher. Other groups brought together people born in the same year. Every society had its meetings and banquets; many of them covered their expenses with income from property given to them or purchased.

The villages thus concealed under a drab and monotonous

Fig. 15.7 An abandoned fortified village in Kansu (from Castell, *Chinaflug*). Evidence of the insecurity formerly associated with this frontier zone

appearance an intense social life. Here the peasant found a thousand opportunities for gossip, discussion, intrigue and the pursuit of common interests.

VILLAGE GOVERNMENT

The government of the Japanese village is simple, at least in appearance: universal suffrage, a municipal council and a mayor. But in practice one must take into account the influence of certain families, affinities between individuals, political slants and religious tendencies, all of which open the way for a multitude of subtle variations.

In the Chinese communities, authority was formerly vested in an ill-defined council of individuals selected on grounds of age, wealth and literacy; these generally elderly notables governed the community in accordance with tradition, and were ill-adapted to deal with new circumstances. Since there was no method of procedure, and no organised voting, confused situations arose that necessitated long palavers. Yet within the framework of custom and tradition, these councils succeeded in maintaining order in the village and in suppressing quarrels. Their endeavour was to mediate in disputes before the latter could be brought before the mandarin tribunal, so as to protect the autonomy of the village from the intrusion of the mandarins and thus defend the interests of the villagers. For to have recourse to mandarin justice was a ruinous procedure; far better to box the whole affair up within the village than to get a considered verdict from a mandarin judge. Besides, in the old China it was the wish of the state that mandarin justice should be hard and expensive, in order to make disputants settle their differences for themselves. If a haggling peasant persisted in his intention to bring his complaint before the mandarin authorities, negotiators supported by the village council (who were not discouraged by their previous unsuccessful attempts to bring about a settlement) would intervene once more to show the complainant where his true interest lay and to try to find a solution that would be face-saving for both parties. If it were a matter of civil proceedings, with no question of punishing a criminal but only of compensating a plaintiff who had been wronged, this conception of justice, with its emphasis on compromise and on the 'face' of both parties, was by no means inappropriate.

It would sometimes happen that a village was plagued by a ruthless individual whose brutality, liability to take offence, and genius for intrigue made him universally feared. Such a person would be feared even more if he were the appointed secret agent of the sub-prefect, to whom he would report possible legal proceedings that might yield substantial bribes. This village swashbuckler was also feared because of his dealings with bands of robbers whom he guided to appropriate victims.

The organisation of the Vietnamese village was much clearer than that of the Chinese village. The council of elders that controlled it was constituted according to recognised rules. All men aged sixty and over were on the council, collaborating with those whose merit had put them there at an earlier age. In principle, therefore, no inhabitant was precluded from taking part in the affairs of the community. The administration of the community, under the control of the council, was entrusted to certain officers, of whom the most important, called rather inaccurately. the mayor, was simply an agent, who had no say in the decisions of the council. The system was flexible, and functioned honourably, reconciling the egalitarianism of the peasants with the acceptance of the hierarchy.

CHAPTER 16

CHANGES IN CIVILISATION AND CHANGES IN RURAL LANDSCAPES

The world is well aware that he who takes a step will accomplish more.

One preference must of necessity be absorbed by another, one set of cultures will lead to another, and there is no end to this process.

Fontenelle

COMMUNIST CHINA AND THE RURAL PAST

China provides an example of changing rural landscapes resulting from the transformation of the basic elements of civilisation. The structure of the human geography is thus clearly revealed: on the one hand, the influences of physical conditions continue to be felt (floods and droughts have hindered agricultural prosperity since 1949), on the other, the legacy of the traditional civilisation continues to weigh very heavily on the presentday human geography. Modern China has a 1000-year inheritance of high rural population densities and an agricultural technique of which account must be taken. Manual operations, ensuring good harvests but very poor wages, continue to be the general rule. It must be stressed that the Chinese countrysides have never before contained so many people. In the old China of the eighteen provinces the total population in 1970 was about 550 million; in 1953 no less than 86 per cent of the then total lived in the rural areas. The total population is growing at the rate of 1.5 per cent per annum, or 8 million a year for the eighteen provinces and 12 million for the whole of China, which, excluding Taiwan, had a population in 1970 of about 750 million.[1] The authorities have engaged in much displacement of labour for the execution of great collective enterprises, but they want the rural people to retain their homes in the countryside. They do not, in other words, favour a spontaneous rural exodus; they noted with regret such an exodus in 1956 and 1957. In Fukien, for example, the *hsien* of Min Hu lost 13 per cent of its active population; 17 000 workers infiltrated into the cities of Fuchow, Nan Ping, and Ku Tien. Other examples (from the same years 1956–57) were the 205 000 peasants who moved into Tientsin, with 500 000 into the metropolitan area of Shanghai and 30 000 into Canton. Such movements would seem to be linked with increasing rural poverty.

Present day technology is still largely that of the past. In 1970, men still bore rickshaws in the towns, or pedalled 'pedicabs'. It is perhaps surprising not to see horses pulling passenger carts, but that has never been a Chinese custom, for men must be fed rather than animals. In 1964 China possessed only 70 000 agricultural tractors. In the environs of Shanghai, in August 1964, peasants were drying their harvest and threshing it with flails on the tarmac roads – a spectacle that could have been seen in Tonkin in 1935. It shows that these peasants had no threshing machines, and that road traffic was almost non-existent. Never before has human manure been gathered with such zeal. An item in the Peking Opera started a debate on what to do with a jar of urine. Should it be emptied on the family garden or on the communal fields? A pretty problem, of which the solution was in no doubt at all: the contents would go to the commune.

Another heritage from the past is the istence of rural crafts. In 1970 the Chinese plan for industrialisation was concerned less with the creation of great production units than with multiplying

[1] The population of China (excluding Taiwan) is not accurately known. The last census was in 1953, and demographers regard it as incomplete; since then we have nothing but the estimates of (non-Chinese) demographers, based on projections from a variety of starting points and using growth rates that differ from one author to another, between 1.5 and 2 per cent per annum. It is thus quite impossible to say whether, at the end of 1970, mainland China (excluding Taiwan and all the Chinese living abroad) had 750 million, 800 million or even 900 million people.

small electric power stations (hydroelectric especially) and small factories, so as to prevent some parts of the country from falling behind. In other words, the wide dissemination of small units. An example is provided by the province of Honan, in which 40 per cent of all the districts now have a chemical fertiliser factory.

Much of the legacy of the traditional civilisation thus remains in the rural landscape: dense populations, primitive technology and small industries. Villages and hamlets have not been abolished; they are still there, inhabited by the same families as in 1949; the working party, the basic unit of agricultural labour, comprises the agricultural labourers of a village or hamlet.

THE COMMUNIST REVOLUTION

The communist regime, however, has undertaken to revolutionise the Chinese countryside. It must be admitted that it was in great need of transformation, having suffered much from the customary routines. The destruction of the clans and of the extended families, and of the authority of the elders, diminished authority of the father of the family, and the suppression of private property have allowed new techniques to be introduced into the countryside — though only in a small way as yet, as noted above. One example is outstanding: the Chinese country-side had inherited from its long past the cultivation of only a small part of the entire area; the greater part of the territory, hills and mountains, was unused, producing neither wood nor forage. This situation had become ossified to such an extent that it was difficult to devise plans for altering it. How could the peasants be induced to change their attitude towards hillsides and mountains, and to respect reafforestation and the planting of orchards? Three-quarters of the area of China (the eighteen provinces) could be made productive by such uses. True, reafforestation could hardly be expected to solve the rural problems, but at least it could materially enlarge the economic horizon of the peasants.

The main benefit of the communist regime has been the estab-lishment of a new order in the countryside. Communist control, starting from the situation inherited from the old China, has per-mitted certain reforms that have had happy results; the collective organisation of agricultural labour has provided the means of rationalising the traditional intensive use of manpower, so as to get even more labour into agriculture and increase the harvests. It has been possible to improve the agricultural water supply situation, which was very necessary; further developments in this direction offer immense possibilities.

It is not certain that the Chinese countryside needed a communist agrarian system. But it certainly needed reorganisation, and it is not farfetched to suggest that only the communists were capable of achieving this. Using the confidence (the Command from Heaven!) the respect and the fear that they inspired, they have overthrown Chinese society and changed the agrarian structure. Although the general aspect of the rural landscape has changed little as yet, new features of considerable consequence have been introduced. The suppression of the old fragmentation and the establishment of a system of large fields, according to the availability of mechanical equipment and the suitability of the land, cannot fail to alter the rural landscape, in the sense of making it simpler and more monotonous. Large water-supply works, as in Anhwei, have created entirely new landscapes. The same is true of areas like eastern Tibet and Sin Kiang, into which Chinese colonisation, well organised, has penetrated. Afforestation of hills and mountains is also transforming the landscape.

THE PEOPLE'S COMMUNES

After a first stage in which the people's communes tried to be phalansteries in which work and services were done in common, some modifications have been introduced by those in control. Agricultural work is now on a collective basis, and the remuneration of workers is in accordance with the tasks accomplished; the rural people are constrained to show great deference to the suggestions of the communist party, but the cultivator has the right to a small plot, the harvest from which he can keep or sell, and furthermore there is no proscription of normal family life. The workers can take their meals at home, at least in the evening. Maternal tasks have been lightened, however, for babies can be left in crèches during the day. But female labour has not greatly diminished, and indeed women work harder than before, either in the fields or in the local factories.

The people's commune has become a sort of administrative unit comprising between 20 000 and 50 000 inhabitants. In the town that acts as headquarters of the commune there will be administrative buildings, repair shops, small industries (fertilisers, bricks, pottery, etc.,) and secondary schools. The 'brigades' own machines and draught animals, and distribute the tasks among the various work gangs that are the real labour units.

SOME EXAMPLES

Some examples of people's communes may enable us to measure the extent and the limits of the modifications made in the relation between man and the environment by the communist revolution.

1. The people's commune of Hong Kiao, some 15 km southwest of Shanghai,[1] has 19 500 inhabitants (in 4500 families) of whom 10 000 are workers. The area cultivated is 11 km², and the density of population is 1772 persons per km² of cultivated land. This high density is explained by the proximity of Shanghai; the commune lies in the market-gardening belt, and there is intensive cultivation of cucumbers, peppers, aubergines, pumpkins, green beans, melons and watermelons. The yield of vegetables per hectare is 82 000 kg — a figure far in excess of the yield in 1949, which was only 33 000 kg. This result has been obtained through more intensive and more scientific cultivation. But the labour is still essentially manual and the manure organic. Human manure is transported in containers suspended from a yoke, and is spread with a shovel or ladle. Systematic pig-rearing produces 15 000 saleable animals a year; the pigs are fattened in communal piggeries, controlled by two vets.

The population is divided into fifteen brigades and 105 work gangs. Each gang corresponds roughly to a former village or hamlet. The improvement of techniques (of irrigation in

[1] J. Chauviré, 'Deux communes populaires chinoises compte rendu de visite', *Bull. Sect. de Géog. Comité des Travaux historiques et scientifiques*, **79**, 1966, 227–57.

particular, which is now done by electric pumps) has contributed to the material improvement in the peasants' living standards; to his agricultural wage the peasant can add the produce of his own garden (44 m² per person) and the breeding of angora rabbits. A worker earns about 600 yuan a year (in 1964 this was worth 1200 new French francs, or £90 sterling); with an average of two workers per family, this means an income of 2400 NF a year (to which must be added free housing, often in the inherited family dwelling, and the value of the garden produce consumed or sold). What is the real value of all this? In this commune rice must be purchased, and this amounts to 8 yuan per person per month (96 yuan a year); and as the average family size is 4.33 persons, the annual expenditure on rice is 416 yuan, against a total yearly income of 1200 yuan (plus the income from the family garden). The spending of 35 per cent of the family income on rice alone is an indication of the low standard of living. On the other hand the large number of bicycles (6000 in the commune) and of watches is an encouraging sign of improvement.

2.　The people's communes in the delta of the Si Kiang, studied by Buchanan,[1] have the advantage, like Hong Kiao, of a suburban situation, with all the opportunities that this offers for the production of profitable crops like vegetables. Furthermore, again as in Hong Kiao, the land is deltaic and therefore fertile and easy to irrigate. The cities that give life to the communes of the Si Kiang delta are Canton and especially Hong Kong, whose 4 million inhabitants provide an enormous market for vegetables, fruit and meat.

Here also it may be observed that the communist revolution has not abolished the old rural landscape, but has modified it through improved techniques and higher yields. The four communes in question cultivated 15 200 hectares, and had 176 500 inhabitants in 1965; the density was thus 1161 per km² of cultivated land. The population benefits from cash sent home by relatives living abroad (in one commune such sums amounted to 10 per cent of the total income) and from the profit of several craft industries. However, for the communes as a whole nine-

---

[1] K. Buchanan, 'The people's communes after six years', *Pacific Viewpoint*, May 1965, pp. 52—64.

tenths of the income is derived from agriculture, animals and fish-farming.

The commune of Cha Chiao, with 4400 ha and 55 700 inhabitants, has an 'agricultural' density of 1250. It specialises in certain commercial activities, and produces almost none of its own food supply; almost the whole of its surface is occupied by fishponds and sugarcane, and it sells 16 000 pigs a year.

The commune of Chin Giao (3200 ha, 45 000 inhabitants, agricultural density 1400) has very varied activities, which explains its high population density per hectare of cultivated land. Most of the area is occupied by sugarcane, vegetables, flowers and fishponds; and there is a yearly sale of 10 000 pigs and the produce of 1500 beehives. Something quite new is the stable-feeding of 600 cows, the milk from which is sold in Canton.

The commune of Chang Cha (1600 ha, 24 500 inhabitants, 1530 per km² of cultivated land) uses half its area for rice, with two harvests a year, a quarter for fishponds, and the remainder (which explains the very high population density) for vegetables for the Canton market. It also produces 5000 pigs a year.

Fa Tung is a commune quite different from the others; its cultivated area only amounts to 6000 ha out of 20 000 ha; the rest of the area is hilly, and virtually unexploited. The 6000 ha of cultivation lie in the alluvial fingers of the delta. These less favourable conditions, and in particular the risk of having no water for the ricefields, explain why the density of population per km² of cultivated land is only 850. Fa Tung produces little but rice and pigs.

Without any doubt, the productivity of these communes, well placed for selling high-priced produce in the markets of Canton and Hong Kong, has been improved by improvements in the techniques of production. Not revolutionary upsets, but just substantial progress. It would be of no advantage to substitute the tractor for the buffalo, but better water control (through canals, dykes, reservoirs, electric pumps, and drainage) gives very profitable returns. The rational use of Canton's night-soil makes for high yields; the cultivators of Chang Cha fashion river-mud into bricks, which they then dry and keep sheltered from the rain until such time as it is convenient to spread them over the fields.

Technical progress has been possible owing to the high degree of organisation already referred to: 4 communes, 78 brigades and 1312 work gangs. The people's commune controls the general direction of affairs, the finance, the trade, the industrial management and the planning. The brigade controls the work gangs and comes to the aid of those that fail to complete their tasks; it is also responsible for primary education and social questions. The work gang is the real labour force. It operates within a framework of contracts passed on by the brigade. The individual peasant within this small group feels the effectiveness of his efforts and the reality of his earnings. It is possible for the annual income of a worker (including all his consumption) to rise to 700 yuan, or even to 1400 yuan. A family with two workers could thus realise an income of 2800 yuan, plus the produce of a garden 300 or 400 square metres in size.

3.   It is probable that the communes in the environs of Canton (and Hong Kong) and Shanghai are exceptionally favoured. A commune in the south of Honan appears much less prosperous.[1] It has 5000 families divided into twenty brigades; each brigade has six to eight work gangs. The village studied (Nan Tsun) had two gangs. A gang incorporated thirty-five families and looked after a defined area. The investigation, made in 1964, yielded the following results: the commune can be reached by a motorable road, and by telephone; the harvest yields have been increased as a result of better irrigation; the workers are paid on the basis of work done, and by the sharing of what remains at the end of the year, after all the gang's expenses have been met (though it must be admitted that there is little to share, for the state quota, taxes, administrative and marketing expenses, and the cost of fertilisers and materials absorb almost all the income). The peasant, thanks to his personal garden, may sell his surplus vegetables, a few chickens, or a pig; but he remains poor and lacking in life's necessities; cloth is rationed and he can hardly clothe himself as he would wish, even if he had the money.

---

[1] P. A. True, 'Nan Tsun, an example of changing units of rural organisation in mainland China', in Thoman and Ratton, *Focus on Geographic Activity*, New York, 1964, pp. 19–26.

SOME WEAKNESSES

China has not yet the means to undertake a technological revolution in the Japanese manner. A new rural China cannot be built, except on the basis of the social structure and technology of the traditional China. Of this simple truth the directors of Chinese agriculture are well aware; the density of the agricultural population, the unstinted and careful use of human labour, and the utilisation of human manure are some of the manifestations of an inevitable human continuity. This is understandable. What is rather less so is the insistence that everything can be done at once and that all can be changed in next to no time. Where lies the error? In taking account of the heritage of the past, or in preaching total and immediate revolution?

The weight of the past is so heavy that precipitate measures, taking insufficient cognisance of the heritage of traditional technology, can cause very real damage. Did not the Central Committee, taking on trust the inaccurate harvest data for 1958, order a reduction in the area under cereals in 1959? Only to create a famine in 1960. Vast irrigation works in northwestern China have not given anything like the results forecast, for the soil rapidly became alkaline. This could, and should, have been foreseen, and measures taken to prevent such a disastrous train of events. A national campaign for the elimination of the sparrow (which was accused of devouring standing grain crops) had to be suddenly broken off when it was realised that the birds had some value in the control of insect life.

A more serious indictment concerns the import of grain. Between 1961 and 1965 China purchased between 5 and 6 million tons of grain a year. This cost 400 million dollars in 1964, and half of it came from non-communist countries. So much less money available for the purchase of equipment, of which the Chinese countryside stands so much in need. This is indeed a proof that Chinese agricultural production is not without its weaknesses.

PAST AND PRESENT IN THE JAPANESE RURAL LANDSCAPE

Relations between man and the land have been profoundly

modified in Japan, not by any transformation of the physical environment but simply by a technological revolution. Here is one more proof of the dominant role played by civilisation in creating the human landscapes of the Far East.

The traditional civilisation had bequeathed to modern Japan an extremely dense peasant population which, from sheer demographic pressure, was forced to cultivate very tiny properties. This effect of history has not been abolished; despite the agrarian reforms of 1946 the average size of a rural farm is still only one hectare. It is impossible to make it larger; the reform has increased the amount of owner occupation but has been unable to increase the size of the farms.

The traditional civilisation has also left Japan with a well-organised and disciplined rural population. From the days of the Meiji the Japanese peasant was surrounded by the severe restraints imposed upon him by the state, the nobility and the village authorities. Before 1868 a peasant was not allowed to go outside his own village, even for a few hours; the penalty was a flogging. There was a very strict etiquette of language and conduct. One's superior must be obeyed, and with a good grace; any show of ill-will was considered as an insult, and true submission must be indicated by gentleness of voice and a smile. A samurai had the right to beat a peasant who violated the rules of etiquette. All the details of what the peasants might consume were precisely laid down by the law; a cultivator who derived an income from 100 kokus of rice (1 koku equalled 180 litres) had the right to construct a house 60 feet long; but he was not permitted to have a room with an alcove, or to have a tiled roof. At the marriage feast of his son or daughter, the quality and quantity of the soup, meat, fish and sweetmeats were fixed by law. The law similarly controlled the price of the presents that might be given to the bride; wine, rice, salted fish; and she could only receive one fan, to cost not more than a certain price. The 100-koku peasant was not allowed to give expensive presents to his friends; the viands that he could offer at funeral feasts must be very simple, and if he served saké it must not be poured into wine glasses but into soup bowls. He was not allowed to wear silk clothes. When a birth occurred in such a family, the grandparents could only offer four presents, the price of which would be limited. And on the boys' feast-day, the lads in a 100-koku family were allowed to receive only a paper flag and two small lances.

The outgoings of a 50-koku family were controlled at a lower level. And as for a 20-koku peasant, his house could not be longer than 36 feet, and it must not be built of expensive woods; at his daughter's wedding-feast he must not serve fish or roast meat, and the female members of his family must not wear leather sandals nor use combs made of tortoiseshell or ivory; the men could not wear stockings, nor leather shoes; they were not allowed to have umbrellas made of oiled paper, and to protect themselves from the rain they must be content with a cloak made of straw. These very stifling customs were severly applied by the government of the Tokugawa shogun family.

A past like this has left its traces: the Japanese cultivator meekly accepts the directives given him by the cooperatives and government organisations. At the instance of the authorities, and in compliance therewith, the Japanese peasants receive a solid education. They attend school for nine years at least, and as part of their instruction read the agricultural papers to keep in touch with technical progress. On an average, every farm manager reads at least half a dozen specialist agricultural periodicals a month. Furthermore, the peasants are 'officered' by agricultural technicians (one to every seven farms), who spread knowledge of technological progress. The cooperatives, uniting all the peasants, help in the diffusion of technical developments, as well as performing their usual functions in the matter of credit, insurance, purchases and sales.

The traditional civilisation has bequeathed to modern Japan an agricultural technique oriented especially towards wet rice cultivation, with little concern for pastoral activities. Formerly the Japanese diet consisted almost entirely of rice, providing carbohydrates, and fish, giving animal protein. To a large extent this is still true. Modern Japan maintains its preference for rice cultivation, and thus for the lowest and flattest lands, most easily adaptable as flooded paddyfields. The area cropped (either once or twice a year) is only 5.2 million hectares, which is no more than one hectare for eighteen inhabitants. But thanks to increased yields the crop more than suffices for Japanese consumption, and by the end of 1969 a stock of nearly 6 million tons of rice had accumulated, which was difficult to dispose of, the price of Japanese rice being above the general world level.

The increased yield of paddy has been obtained by scientific selection, by a manuring programme based on careful experimentation (and the almost complete abandonment of human manure), by the careful and precise organisation of irrigation, by a successful campaign against diseases, and by very careful weeding. In the most northerly parts of Japan the seedbeds are protected from frost by sheets of plastic; this practice alone has increased the average yield by about 13 per cent. It allows the sowing of slower-maturing varieties that are heavier yielders; a seedbed under plastic permits sowing (and thus replanting) fifteen days earlier.

The study of irrigation has shown that total and continuous control of water (that is, watering according to the exact requirements of the moment, without needing to be preoccupied with conserving water in the paddyfield that might be for the time being useless if not actually harmful, but precious in the coming weeks) has raised the national average yield of rice, already very high at 5000 kg per hectare, by 20 per cent. An excellent example of the subtlety of irrigation technique is to be found in the northern islands of the archipelago; here the yields are reduced by the coldness of the irrigation water that enters the paddyfields (for if the water temperature is less than 15°C the yield is 30 per cent less near to the outlet of the pipe supplying the water). To overcome this difficulty, the incoming water is led through a long pipe pierced with small holes, so that it mingles slowly, and over a long distance, with the water already in the field.

The Japanese peasantry, faithful to its tradition, does not seek to establish alpine pastures in the mountains. There is still some shifting cultivation, but no real pastoral activity. Japan is increasing her production of eggs, milk and meat, but this is through technologically advanced enterprises, using feedstuffs purchased from specialist factories.

There is one novel aspect of rural Japan; it is no longer the essential Japan, for the rural population is only 30 per cent of the total, and the remaining 70 per cent live in the towns and cities. Further, the rural population are no longer exclusively cultivators. Many people now living in the rural areas are industrial wage earners, or are employed in the towns, or are in non-agricultural ancillary occupations such as school-teachers, technicians, doctors, nurses or shopkeepers. It is difficult to say just how many active agriculturalists Japan now has; perhaps it was around 10 million in the late 1960s. But of these 10 million, at least half must have been part-time workers.

One other notable change is that the Japanese countryside is becoming motorised. Nearly 2 million motor cultivators are used in the fields, while the farms themselves are almost over-equipped with electrical gadgets such as threshers, huskers, pumps and so on. These mechanical appliances permit a more and more intensive use of the land with less human labour and no draught animals at all; this last is a most important advance in a country with no tradition of meadows and no inclination towards stock-farming.

All in all, the present Japanese rural landscape is unintelligible without careful and continuous reference to its past history; but the fields are being reorganised to accommodate the new technology. The human geography of the Japanese countryside is still a superb example of the landscape-making quality of the civilisation and of the farreaching consequences of changing technology.

BIBLIOGRAPHY

ANDERSSON, J. G. *Children of the Yellow Earth*, London, 1934.

ARAKAWA, H. 'Climates of Northern and Eastern Asia', in Landsberg, *World Survey of Climatology*, vol. viii, 1969.

BALAZS, E. *La Bureaucratie céleste*, Paris, 1968.

BOULBET, J. 'Le Miir, culture itinérante avec jachère forestière en pays Maá. Région de Blao. Bassin du fleuve Daá Dööng (*Dông Nai*)', *Bulletin Ecole française Extrème-Orient*, 53, No. 1, 1966, 77—88.

BRUNEAU, M. 'Villages du Nord-Ouest de la Thailande, étude géographique', *Bull. Sect. de Géog.*, *Comité des Travaux historiques et scientifiques*, 79, 1966, 25—42.

BRUZON and CARTON, *Le Climat de l'Indochine et les typhons de la Mer de Chine*, Hanoi, 1939.

BUCHANAN, K. *The transformation of the Chinese Earth*, London, 1970.

BUCHANAN, K. 'The people's communes after six years', *Pacific Viewpoint*, May 1965, 52—64.

BUCK, J. L. *Chinese Farm Economy*, Chicago, 1930.

BUCK, J. L. *Land Utilization in China*, Shanghai, 1937.

CASTELL, GRAF zu *Chinaflug*, Berlin, 1938.

CHAUVIRE, J. 'Deux communes populaires chinoises: compte rendu de visite', *Bull. Sect. de Géog.*, *Comité des Travaux historiques et scientifiques*, 79, 1966, 227—57.

CHEN FOU. *Récits d'une vie fugitive, mémoires d'un lettré pauvre*, Paris, 1967.

CORNELL, J. B. and SMITH, R. J. *Two Japanese Villages: Matsunagi, a japanese mountain community; Kurusu, a japanese agricultural community*, Ann Arbor, 1956.

CRESSEY, G. B. 'The Fenghsien landscape; a fragment of the Yangtse Delta', *Geographical Review*, 1936, 396—413.

DELVERT, J. *Le Paysan cambodgien*, Paris, 1961.

DERRUAU, M. *Le Japon*, Paris, 1967.

DUPUIS, J. *L'Asie méridionale*, Paris, 1969.

EBERHARD, W. *Settlement and Social Change in Asia*, London, 1967.

EMBREE, J. F. *A Japanese Village, Suye Mura*, London, 1946.

FITZGERALD, C. P. *The Tower of Five Glories, a study of the Min Chid of Ta Li, Yunnan*, London, 1941.

FREEBERNE, M. 'Natural calamities in China, 1949—1961: an examination of the reports originating from the mainland', *Pacific Viewpoint*, 1962, 33—72.

FREEDMAN, R. and MULLER, J. 'The continuing fertility decline in Taiwan', 1965, *Popul. Index*, 33, No. 1, 3—17.

GOUROU, P. *Les Paysans du Delta tonkinois*, Paris, 1936.

GOUROU, P. *L'Habitation annamite en Annam septentrional et central*, Paris, 1936.

GOUROU, P. *L'Utilisation du sol en Indochine français*, Paris, 1940.

GOUROU, P. 'La population rurale de la Cochinechinc', *Annales de Géographie*, 1942, 7—25.

GOUROU, P. 'Civilisation et géographie humaine en Asie des Moussons', *Bulletin Ecole française Extrême-Orient*, 44, No. 2, 1954, 467—76.

GOUROU, P. *L'Asie*, Paris, 1964.

GRANET, M. *La Civilisation chinoise*, Paris, 1929.

GRANET, M. *La Pensée chinoise*, Paris, 1934.

HENDRY, J. B. *The Small World of Khanh Hâu*, Chicago, 1964.

HOMMEL, R. P. *China at Work*, New York, 1937.

HOON, K. LEE. *Land Utilization and rural economy in Korea*, Shanghai, 1936.

HORNELL, J. *Water Transport*, London, 1946.

HSIANO TUNG FUI. *Peasant Life in China*, London, 1939.

IZIKOWITZ, K. G. *Lamet, hill peasants in French Indochina*, Göteborg, Etnologiska Studier, 1951, 275.

KELLING, R. *Das Chinesiche Wohnhaus*, Tokyo, 1935.

KING, F. H. *Farmers of Forty Centuries*, New York, 1926.

KUNSTADTER, P., ed., *Southeast Asian Tribes, Minorities and Nations*, Princeton, 1967.

LAUTENSACH, H. *Korea*, Leipzig, 1945.

LI MING CHUNG *Construction in the Song Period*, 3 vols (in Chinese), Shanghai, 1912, 1923, 1929.

MATSUDAIRA, N. *Etude sociologique sur les fêtes saisonnières dans la province de Mikawa*, Paris, 1936.

NEEDHAM, J. *Science and civilisation in China*, Cambridge, 5 vols, 1956, *et seq.*

NEVILLE, W. 'Singapore: ethnic diversity and its implications', *Ann. Assoc. Amer. Geogr.*, 1966, 56, No. 2, 136–253.

OLIVER, J. 'Bamboo as an economic resource in Southern Asia', *Geography*, 41, 1956, 49–56.

PERNY, PAUL *Proverbes chinois*, Paris, 1869.

PEZEU-MASSABUAU, J. 'La maison traditionnelle au Japon', *Cahiers d'Outre-Mer*, 1916, 293–7.

PEZEU-MASSABUAU, J. 'La maison japonaise et la neige', Paris, *Bulletin de la Maison franco-japonaise*, 1966.

PEZEU-MASSABUAU, J. *Géographie du Japon*, Paris, 1968.

PEZEU-MASSABUAU, J. 'Les problèmes géographiques de la maison chinoise', *Cahiers d'Outre-Mer*, 1970, 252–83.

SPENCER, J. E. 'Chinese place-names and the appreciation of geographic realities', *Geographical Review*, 1941, 79–94.

TADAO KANO and KOKICHI SEGAWA, *An Illustrated Ethnography of Formosan Aborigines: 1. The Yami*, Tokyo, 1956.

TAWNEY, R. H. *Agrarian China*, London, 1939.

TRUE, P. A. 'Nan Tsun, an example of changing units of rural organisation in mainland China', in Thoman and Ratton, eds, *Focus on Geographic Activity*, New York, 1964, 19–26.

VANDER MEERSCH, LÉON. *La Formation du légisme: recherche sur la constitution d'une philosophie politique caractéristique de la Chine ancienne*, Paris, EFEO 1965, 56.

YANG, L. S. *Les Aspects économiques des Travaux publics dans la Chine impériale*, Paris, 1964.

YOSHIDA, T. *Das Japanische Wohnhaus*, Berlin, 1935.

INDEX